THE POWER OF
PARENTAL INFLUENCE

TIMOTHY CHAPMAN,
Msc.D., C.S.A.C.

America's Parenting Coach

Illustrations by Yuri Elvin

VERBA VOLENT, SCRIPTA MANENT
Celerus Books
AN IMPRINT OF FIDELI PUBLISHING, INC.

Celerus is an imprint of Fideli Publishing
www.fidelipublishing.com

ISBN: 978-1-60414-158-0

Table of Contents

Introduction
Six Words That Will Change Everything

Emerging Adulthood is the new period of time between adolescence and adulthood. The transition into adulthood has changed. Not everyone makes it successfully, and it's usually for emotional reasons. I call them "midolescents." They are stuck and need help. The solution lies in six simple words that are the foundation of this book and the key aspect to what I call the Art of Feeling.

Chapter 1
Emerging Midolescence

The midolescent emerges from adolescence. He looks like an adult but expresses himself emotionally and behaviorally like a teenager. Why does this happen and what can be done about it? This chapter follows the arc of the midolescent and his relationships with his parents. The roots of midolescence are found in the unresolved issues of the adolescent.

Chapter 2
Why is Adolescence So Tough Today?

The roots of the midolescent epidemic are found deep in the changes taking place in our society during adolescence. What is normally a time of separating and individuation is now subject to stressors and strains never seen before in any culture.

Chapter 3
Dynamics of a Healthy Family

It's important to understand family dynamics. Where do healthy families get their communication patterns? The same place unhealthy families get theirs: from their parents. This chapter discusses the positive effects upon children when parents express themselves in ways that builds intimacy and trust. It includes case histories and examples.

Chapter 4
Healing the Lifespark

Every child is born with a healthy Lifespark. It contains nine components. Families either nurture or damage the Lifespark in varying degrees. It's important to understand how the Lifespark works and what a parent can do to nurture these nine components in their child. With training, parents can become the best healers of their child's Lifespark.

Chapter 5
Communicating Your Feelings

Parents who model expressing their feelings in a way that does not shame, accuse, or create hysterical situations for their children set a positive example. Over time the healthy expression of emotions will not only resolve a parent's feelings, but will become a method that their kids can follow. Though it may take time, behavior change will generally follow a parent's consistent healthy expression of feelings.

Chapter 6
Re-Directing Your Midolescent

This chapter is your roadmap to success in taking charge as a parent and utilizing the skills you have acquired thus far to re-direct your midolescent's path to adulthood. Here you will decide what unacceptable behaviors have to go and how to make that happen. You will learn to author and negotiate a thirty-day behavioral contract with your midolescent, marking a formal starting point for his growth into adulthood. It teaches parents to never negotiate with their midolescent during a crisis and to renegotiate only after thirty-days of consistent behavior. Parents will list the five things that are most important, not to their child, but to them. The contract is designed to be simple and manageable. By using the Six Basic Feelings, parents can continue to reinforce their midolescent's positive behavior and ultimately redirect their transition into adulthood and out of their house.

Chapter 7
Creating the Controlled Conflict

There can be no growth without conflict. As long as a midolescent is at ease and can continue in his current lifestyle, he's at rest and secure. Once a written contract is enforced and the midolescent feels pressure to change, expect problems. This chapter focuses on how to handle those problems in a variety of scenarios while measuring your success.

Chapter 8
Intervention—When All Else Fails

If you have tried everything outlined in this book and your midolescent won't respond it could be due to extensive drug or alcohol abuse or complicated psychiatric conditions. In either case, drastic behavior requires a rapid response. There is still hope, but you must act now. It's called intervention.

Epilogue: Why I Wrote This Book

Appendix 1: Assessment Guides for Teenage Behavior

Appendix 2: Worksheet for Examining and Developing a Behavior Contract

Citations

Poster: Six Basic Feelings (to hang in your home)

Illustrations: Yuri Elvin.................. Yurielvin@yahoo.com

Author: Timothy Chapman .... tim@teensavers.com

Introduction

Six Words That Will Change Everything

If you are reading this book, chances are you are one of the millions of parents in America who have an out of control adolescent or midolescent. You're probably wondering, "What is midolescence?" Sociologists and psychologists have confirmed what I have been seeing for the last two decades in my practice. Our society, for a variety of reasons, has dropped in a new aging period in between adolescence and adulthood. They call this "emerging adulthood." It is not necessarily a time of unhealthy behavior, but a maturing pattern that is distinct from the past. Adulthood no longer takes place automatically at eighteen or nineteen, but during this new period of emerging adulthood that can last well into the late twenties and early thirties. Kids are extending their education, shopping around for careers, trying different jobs, dating more, or not dating at all. They are doing a variety of things, but most of all they are postponing the traditional choices of adulthood—marriage, family, and career. As a result, they are dependent on their parents longer and are more unsettled than in past generations. The good news is that most of them move on into healthy adulthood. The bad news is a considerable number don't. I call these kids who have a difficult time making the leap into adulthood "midolescents." They live in a nebulous middle ground between adolescence and adulthood, and they tend to do it on their parents' dime.

They are adults physically, but they behave like adolescents. They have transitioned through their adolescence chronologically but not emotionally. If you have one living at home, you know exactly what I'm talking about. Midolescence is rooted in adolescence, which is a normal period of time between the innocence of childhood and maturity of adulthood. It is an important period that must be transited properly or it will derail their future development into productive adulthood. During this period, which is characterized by separation from their parents and growth into distinct individuals, some kids get stuck. They have suffered an interruption in their growth process. If your child is a midolescent, you are faced with an angry, sullen or apathetic young adult who lacks motivation and just won't or can't grow-up.

You are probably wondering what happened to your family. Do all parents go through this agony? Growing up in our culture today is tough. Our children are faced with challenges that we as children never faced. And now one of our greatest tasks as parents is not to become another of their challenges. Parents have limited options for dealing with their adolescents and less in dealing with their midolescents. They are forced to "feel" their way through this period in their child's life. Rules and methods that worked in other stages of their lives go out the window. A new period of transition has begun, and for some kids chaos sets in.

This book covers what happens when a child grows out of adolescence chronologically but never matures emotionally and falls into this midolescent state. They are easy to spot. They have the body of an adult but the feelings and emotional maturity of a thirteen-year-old. They can be anywhere between the ages of eighteen to twenty-eight or older, but they deal with life's difficulties with the maturity of a teen or pre-teen. Our society is suffering through a crisis wave of midolescent youth. Both boys and girls are stuck emotionally because they have not developed the internal tools necessary to grow-up into fully functioning adults.

The method I have successfully used for the past thirty-years, and which I will teach you in this book, will help get your child over the midolescent hump into fully functioning adulthood. I call this method the Art of Feeling and at its core are six words (mad-sad-glad- afraid-ashamed-hurt). Once you learn their power and how to use them, I am convinced they will change how you behave in your important relationships. These six words will become your strongest ally when dealing with your adult child. They have helped thousands of parents, and have saved a few of their lives as well. You can be successful as a parent. Your children do not have to stay stuck in their immaturity and rebellion. How did they get that way?

Adolescents' emotional and psychological make-up has not changed all that much during the past century, yet the world around them has transformed from one of dirt roads and horseless carriages to one of instant messaging the space station as it orbits overhead. The possibilities and influences on our children are almost endless, and many of them are beyond the control of the average parent. The onset of puberty can happen three to five years earlier than at the turn of the century. Peer pressure, self-esteem, dating, school, have all changed dramatically, making life more exciting yet challenging for our kids and putting parents in difficult situations.

Today's parents are, for the most part, ill-equipped to deal with the changes affecting their children. Parents are challenged by their teenagers in ways never before imagined. Technology has made us truly global and lazy. Our neighborhoods are no longer what they once were. Extended family has lost its importance. Living nearby is no longer necessary in order to stay in touch with friends and relatives. We drive more than we walk. We eat fast food instead of health food. We habitually drink diet soda and coffee that is ten to fifty times stronger than the coffee our parents or grandparents drank. Everything is convenient, yet we are always in a hurry. Everybody's rushed, yet we're running late. We know more people than our parents could ever have dreamt of meeting, yet we are lonelier than we have ever been.

Despite all this distraction, the opportunity to connect with your children is as possible today as any time in history. Parents have a void to fill too. What I will teach you in this book will help you as much as it will help your children. In many ways, these lessons can become your saving grace.

Children are complicated. Their outside world may have changed, but two things will never change. First, kids are going to push limits as they have always done. Second, parents must invest time and emotional energy into them more so now than ever before. Time is not on your side.

Reading this book is an investment in your child's life that will be rewarded in the long term. I have compiled in these pages over thirty-years of expertise and experience working with adolescents, midolescents, and their parents. Information here is professional, practical, and effective. Hundreds of health care professionals have contributed to this book. And you are the beneficiary.

I ask that while you read, please memorize the Six Basic Feelings I am about to introduce to you, and practice them with the exercises I have included. By doing so, you will be astonished at the way you react toward your child. Your child will be amazed as well.

As a metaphysician, counselor and teacher, I believe anything is possible. I believe people are generally good and want to do good for others. This includes adolescents and their older manifestation, the midolescent.

I invite you to sit back, grab a cup of coffee or tea, take a breath and read your way into the new world of relating to and understanding your adolescent and midolescent children.

Thanks for picking up my book.

Timothy Chapman, Msc.D. C.S.A.C.

Chapter One

Emerging Midolescence
The Midolescent Child

The end of adolescence used to clearly mark the transition from childhood into adulthood. But in the last few decades a cultural shift has taken place in our country in the way eighteen to thirty-year-olds mature into functional adults. Because of changes in child-labor laws, mass education, and other social and institutional factors, a whole new and distinct stage of life has developed that is situated between the adolescent period and adulthood. They now call this age group "emerging adulthood."[1] Part of the influence of this "emerging adulthood" is the structural change in the American economy. Young adults are pressured to postpone career choices and even marriage in order to pursue expanded educational opportunities. They no longer settle into stable careers at eighteen and often go through a period of extended education even into graduate school. It is acceptable and often necessary to wander from job-to-job to find where one fits in. These emerging adults are postponing marriage late into their twenties and even their thirties.

While the "emerging adult" population continues growing, it is apparent from the behavior patterns

I increasingly see at the Chapman House treatment program that it's easier for many of these young adults to fall through the cracks in our now less structured social fabric. No longer is there a clearly definable transition from child to adulthood. It is acceptable for the process of maturing to linger on for years. For these reasons, I believe it is more difficult than ever for young persons to develop their authentic selves, to find their career, their calling, their place in our society, and to make a successful transition into full adulthood.

If you add to that mix the divorce rate, the increased materialism and the consumerism focused society we live in, along with the rise and influence of an increasingly sophisticated media culture, it is no wonder that the number of young adults who are stuck in what I call "midolescence" continues to grow.

Midolescents are the unmotivated kids, the ones who have not grown out of their ego-centric behavior. They behave and feel like adolescents, but they inhabit adult bodies. I sometimes refer to them as "twenty-six-year old teenagers." All of these young adults suffer from a damaged Lifespark. (We will examine the Lifespark in detail in chapter four.) This damage inhibits them from developing the skills and competence they need to move into adulthood.

Midolescents are stuck with unproductive feelings that do not allow them to move forward in their emotional and social development.

Jeremy is twenty-four and still lives at home with his father and mother, Bill and Colleen. By the time they brought Jeremy in for treatment, he had just admitted to his parents, after Colleen found a bag of marijuana in his clothing, that he'd been smoking it regularly since his sophomore year of high school. For the first time, Bill and Colleen were concerned enough to seek treatment. It had been a long process for them to realize their son needed help.

At first, they didn't mind that Jeremy seemed in no rush to move out. Their intention for him after high school was that he would attend one of several four-year colleges in the area, but Jeremy just never seemed to get it together in high school. He had missed out on some classes and flunked others and didn't qualify for the state college. So Jeremy started at the local junior college, which was still all right with them, but it didn't take long for him to lose interest. He was more intent on attending concerts with his friends, hanging out listening to music, and staying out late. Bill hadn't been big on school when he was young and had worked his way up in a company from a salesman to a corporate executive. So he wasn't adamant that Jeremy pursue high academic achievement, but he expected him to at least work. And it surprised and confused Bill that Jeremy never seemed to get along with his boss or his co-workers or couldn't show up on time and inevitably found himself out of work.

In some ways this really didn't bother Colleen because theirs was a nice upper middle-class lifestyle, so

Jeremy didn't need to help the family or to take care of his own needs. He would "grow up," she often reassured her husband, and eventually find his own way. Besides, Jeremy living at home didn't at all put a strain financially on the family.

All of this did stress Bill's relationship with his son. Despite his inability to talk about his building frustration, he had been concerned about Jeremy as far back as high school. Every time the two had a man-to-man talk about his future, the conversation would degenerate to the point where Bill lost his temper and started accusing Jeremy of being a slacker, at times he jabbing his finger in Jeremy's face and telling him he would never amount to much if he didn't buckle down. This only caused Jeremy to stalk off, slam the door to his room, and turn his music up a decibel level just below a jet engine.

The arguing continued throughout high school and centered on the fact that Jeremy couldn't hold down a job, couldn't complete a task, wasn't motivated to do well enough in school to graduate. If he was going to live in Bill's house, he insisted Jeremy at least hold down a job and stop staying out late with his friends. Each time, Jeremy would grudgingly comply and get a new job, but he either didn't get along with his co-workers, couldn't get to work on time, or just lost interest and either was fired or quit. Colleen would then soothe the situation over by giving Jeremy whatever he needed—usually money for clothes and food.

Bill continued to grow frustrated but he could not have any meaningful discussion with his son without falling into a shouting match. Jeremy and Colleen tiptoed around him until he had pushed down his feelings enough to function in the house without blowing-up.

* * *

This pattern has continued for five or six years now and Bill is ready to do anything to get Jeremy motivated. On the other hand, Colleen is afraid because Jeremy is depressed. When Bill began talking about leaving her if this situation didn't change, Colleen finally insisted they seek help for Jeremy.

* * *

For the first fourteen years of my practice, I worked exclusively with adolescents and their parents. Then parents started bringing their young adults like Jeremy into my office describing family situations like the one above. Kids like Jeremy are the ones I call midolescents. They are no longer considered adolescents because they've grown chronologically past the mythical adult barrier, eighteen years of age, and are well into their twenties. Supposedly they should be well on their way to establishing themselves as productive and responsible adults. Yet Jeremy still acts emotionally and intellectually like a teenager. In my experience, he has not completed the essential growing-up process of his adolescent years. Unfortunately for him and his parents, he does not get a free pass into adulthood despite parental best intentions. But the essential work of separating effectively from his parents and finding his

Lifespark, those elements of individuation that make him truly unique, has not been completed. And worse yet he's stuck—not only in his parents' home without much hope of getting out on his own, but in a cycle of addiction that is a symptom of a deeper problem.

Jeremy is part of a growing number of midolescent adults in our country that exist in a no-man's land of unintentional destiny. We were never designed to live in that middle stage on the cusp of adulthood, having the privileges of an autonomous adult, but none of the inner emotional tools to function as one. That's another reason I call this extended middle passage of adolescence "midolescence."

This midolescent period is characterized by the inability to make the emotional leap to adulthood and by continued dependence on parents for emotional or financial support or both. Since they can't deal with the stresses of growing up, they always suffer some form of addiction.

Over the last fifteen years, almost all of the midolescents I've treated are addicted to alcohol or drugs or both and their emotional life is in an uncontrollable turmoil. From my perspective, it is an epidemic sweeping our society. No one sector of our society—the very affluent, the solidly middle class, or the lower income family—is immune from having one or more of these children in their household. My goal in writing this book is to arm parents, first, with hope. I'm going to teach you proven strategies for circumventing your child's downward spiral into midolescent life. If they are already there, this book will teach you specific skills and remedies I call the Art of Feeling. It's a process consisting of six words that will change everything in your relationships. With some honest work and simple practice, you will be able to use these techniques to facilitate healing in your family. Seeking help for your struggling family will be the best step you will ever make for yourself and your kids.

Getting back to Jeremy, the question is how did he get into this situation? If you were looking from the outside in at this family, they look all-American. Both parents are responsible, ably employed, and possess a nice two-story home with a two-car garage. But what you see is only what Bill and Colleen want their neighbors and co-workers to see. After much counseling, it became abundantly clear to me that Bill had unconsciously passed on his feelings of toxic-shame to his son who had effectively internalized it and was living out the family script to the letter.

My purpose here is not to cast stones at parents by further heaping guilt upon them for their perceived shortcomings. For the most part, by the time parents come into my office the shame and guilt drip from their words and grip their emotions. My heart goes out to them. Yet I know from my years of dealing with these family dynamics that often the parents need as much help as their children.

Let me explain. Raising teens can be turbulent. It is natural for adolescents to have difficulties and for parents to experience frustration. But in my experience a parent's greatest challenge has little to do with their kids and more to do with their own history with their parents. There can be no greater influence, positive or negative, on parents than that of their own parents' style of raising children.

In stressful situations, we often act out of the script we have learned from our parents. These scripts are our internalized feelings linked to the images and scenes from our formative years embedded in our memories. It is very much like how firemen or doctors who one minute are drinking a cup of coffee and talking about the weather, then in the next instant are thrust into life-threatening situations, behave. They react. They are trained to react with professionalism and skill. If they had to stop and look up answers in a book, lives would be lost—maybe even their own. They have internalized their training to the point it becomes one with their personality.

We all behave the same way because it is our nature to do so. According to Silvan Tompkins our feelings are experienced in the context of our biographical experiences, which are the situations and interactions of our lives.[2] These have been encoded in our memory as scenes. Thus, human emotions become the essential motivating force in all human behavior because these biological mechanisms in our brains unfold according to precisely written scripts.

This explains Jeremy's father's behavior. Bill wasn't that good in school or sports and his father openly ridiculed him, telling him often he would never amount to anything if he didn't buckle down. Bill, driven by that shaming, never did do much better in school, but instead became a workaholic. He was out to prove his competency by becoming the top achiever in his sales department. He worked harder and longer than his colleagues, stuffing down his gnawing sense of inadequacy. While not a falling-down drunk, Bill often medicated himself with alcohol after work. But in front of his family, his co-workers, and his fellow church members, he was a man in control. He had learned to effectively hide away his secret self, the part of him that so desperately needed the validation his father wouldn't or couldn't give him. Bill suffered from what best selling author of Bradshaw on the Family and Healing the Shame That Binds, John Bradshaw, calls toxic shame.[3]

At this point you might be asking, wasn't it a good thing Bill was so motivated to achieve? He was probably a boss's delight, a self-motivated man who hit all his numbers, hardly ever called in sick, and never gave any excuses. What's the difference between Bill, a man who is self-motivated to perform in order to meet an unmet-dependency need, and a man who achieves out of enjoyment for what he does? The difference between the two is dramatic: Bill is driven by a need to feel better about himself; the other man is motivated to excellence because he loves what he's doing. These two illustrate the divergent functions of shame.

Not all shame is bad, as John Bradshaw points out in Healing the Shame that Binds You. It is much like the two kinds of cholesterol. HDL is healthy and LDL is toxic. Healthy shame is a human feeling that makes us uniquely human, setting limits and boundaries, letting us know that limitation is our essential nature. Tompkins views shame as an innate feeling that limits our experiences of interest, curiosity, and pleasure. There is no such thing as unlimited human power. We are all faced with our limitations and shortcomings. Healthy people accept their limitations and natural shame acts to put limits in our lives.[4]

On the other hand, when Bill came to accept his father's script that he was internally flawed, toxic-shame became his internalized identity. This "internalization" is a process that takes place over time and includes three dynamics: First, identification with a shame-based model (in this case Bill's father); second, emotional or physical abandonment (Bill's feelings were not mirrored and validated by his parents); third, the interconnection of visual memories and the retaining of shaming-auditory imprints (feelings become imprinted in our memories in the context of our biographical experience). This process took place gradually through Bill's interaction with his family during the pre-adolescent and adolescent period of his maturity. His parents never met Bill's dependency needs by mirroring his feelings, therefore his ego defense mechanism was to convert or transform his developmental needs into workaholism. The real Bill, who has been shamed as defective, goes into hiding at work and doesn't want to come home. At the root of all addiction is toxic-shame, in this case, Bill's workaholism.

Bill functioned fairly well like this in his marriage and on his job. He dealt with the stresses by burying himself in his career. But the stress of raising Jeremy brought to the surface of his life all of his internalized scripts. The harder kids push their parents the faster their unresolved issues come to surface, and this is what happened to Bill as he began to confront his son. When Bill should have been able to listen to his son, offer support and encouragement by mirroring his son's feelings, his only option was to fall back on his training. Whenever he and Jeremy tried to discuss his schoolwork, his future plans, and his lack of motivation to hold down a job the shaming scripts playing in his head dominated the discussions with his son.

Jeremy in turn began to internalize these scripts as well, living them out in his life. The family cycle of shame is passed down to another generation but now with apparently different results, yet all from the same cause. Since Bill was unable to support Jeremy by mirroring and naming his feelings, Jeremy lost touch with his vital-human powers. Since Jeremy is now incapable of accessing his own feelings, he became bonded to his parents' emotions, and he is now unable to separate from his parents. This dependent state is another symptom of midolescence, which again is the extended adolescent middle passage between childhood and adulthood. It is a desert devoid of authentic feelings where increasingly young adults are living, to their great detriment.

As Bradshaw points out, once a child's sense of autonomy is crushed, toxic-shame becomes manifested as either the rebellious child or the total conformist. Once a child's selfhood and personal power are wounded, his drive for autonomy and separateness are bound in toxic-shame. In this case, Jeremy began to look for ways to validate himself with friends, with work, with school—but nothing worked. The rejection from multiple sources of possible influence and validation is stressful for any child. So self-medication for Jeremy was an easy choice since he was exposed early to friends who smoked and drank. It is easier and more satisfying for Jeremy to get high than to experience the pervasive sense of rejection folding into his life. If he didn't have to feel, he wouldn't have to face the details of his life that needed to be worked on for him to separate emotionally from his parents. Since Jeremy never developed the inner emotional resources to respond to the stresses of mature situations, his jump into adulthood is on hold.

Jeremy's mother supported him emotionally by tolerating his outbursts, by cleaning-up after him, and by paying his bills he couldn't take care of himself. She cared for him like the child he still is. Her codependent nature allowed her to fall into this trap of taking care of an adult child.

Bill would love to talk to his son, but he is so out-of-touch with his own feelings, it is difficult for him to even know what he is feeling. How could he help his son through this turbulent time? The thought of being vulnerable regarding his own sense of inadequacy and the toxic-shame he had harbored for years just doesn't enter into the equation as a possibility. It was imperative for Bill to always be in control of himself. So masking how he actually felt was central to his secrecy and the false sense-of-self he had built up and so carefully presented to the world. The cycle of toxic-shame continued until the family pain was too much for them collectively to bear, and that was when they sought out professional help.

By the time they were sitting in my office, Jeremy was deeply entrenched in his midolescent sense of inadequacy and toxic-shame. He had lost all motivation, and he masked his pain by drinking and smoking marijuana until the addicting feelings of euphoria blocked out his driving sense of emptiness and the loneliness that haunted his life. His friends were the only ones who understood him because they willingly accepted another soul into their club of lost children.

I think it is obvious that the roots of the midolescence crisis run deep into the stages of a child's development. A clearer understanding of what transpires during that developmental period will be critical to understanding the causes and remedies of midolescence.

Chapter Two

Why is Adolescence So Tough Today?

Many parents today are in pain because of their relationship with their teens. Teens and preteens are suffering depression, anxiety disorders, substance and alcohol abuse, and unhappiness, particularly among affluent, well-educated families[5], at alarming rates, and parents are alone and ill equipped to help them. Watching your child self-destruct is one of the most painful experiences a parent can go through. The majority of parents I deal with are at a loss as to why, in their seemingly normal homes, where their kids ostensibly have every advantage available to them, they lack motivation, won't obey the rules, take drugs, drink to excess, make foolish and childish choices and just don't get what growing-up is all about. Was adolescence always this difficult? Many parents remember otherwise and are at a loss to understand what has transpired since they were teens.

My experience as a counselor is that parenting today is more difficult than it has ever been. Our culture has undergone a change in the last four or five decades that has solidified into a child-unfriendly environment. Parents have fewer options when it comes to influencing their children. They are out-muscled by the media and a vastly superior technology that is readily available at their children's fingertips. There has never been a time in history when teens have been so assaulted with messages from the media that either conflicts with or outright contradicts what parents are trying to teach their kids. Whether it is from the TV, movies, the Internet, books, or magazines, today's kids are getting a message that is generally at odds with what their parents want for them. The challenges facing parents today are more complex simply because they are thrown into the hormonal mix of the blooming adult world where a new set of expectations is impressed upon their kids from the mass media and reinforced by their peer group.

Children are exposed to violence and sexual behavior through our advanced technology at an earlier and earlier age. Consequently, they lose their sense of innocence earlier than previous generations. In addition, puberty is taking place earlier and the end of adolescence seems to wind on endlessly into their twenties. All of this works to make parenting more challenging than ever before.

The home was once a secure parental domain, and I don't mean that in an authoritative or control sense alone, but the outside sources of influence that challenged the transmission of parental values and structure were limited. There was a time when it was easier to control what came into the home; the pressures and issues from the outside were known and somewhat benign. Those days are gone. The Internet alone presents possibilities for good or bad in the home that a previous generation of parents simply didn't have to deal with. Control over the home environment has steadily eroded on many fronts—in the schools, in the courts, and again by the media and technology. While some outside influences (parental TV control, Homeland Security, metal detectors, and police on campus in our schools) were necessary in order to protect at-risk kids, the sense of power has shifted and parents are at a loss to know what to do. More sophisticated parenting tools are needed now than at any time in history.

I have successfully guided hundreds of parents through these difficult and turbulent times. Whether your child is sixteen or twenty-six, this method works. Hundreds of graduates of my program are leading drug-free, alcohol-free, responsible lives. In this book, I am going to teach you proven methods for reaching your child. I will teach you how to influence them for good whether you think it is possible or not. But I will not sugar coat the process. This book is designed to help you as a parent take stock of where you are as a father or as a mother and do some hard work. Many of the ways you react to your children's behavior and demands have more to say about your own history and the emotional issues in your own life than theirs. I will have a lot to say about that in this book. If you as a parent are clear about what motivates your emotional responses, you will have the power to help your child with theirs. Today the power with our kids is not in controlling them, but in influencing them. You can learn this. You can change the way you react. You can win over the despair and discouragement in your child's life. I am just going to ask you to do one thing.

Don't give up. Keep reading. There is a reason you are in this predicament and I want you to know it is not all your fault.

The New Adolescent

By the time parents bring their kids to me a lot has been said by them that was ineffective, tempers have flared on both sides, maybe even threats were made, hopes and dreams of what having children would be like have diminished, and any sense of innocence in their child's life has been lost forever. There can be no turning back the clock. Their kids have become addicted and are savvy about the world, about sex, about drugs, and they think their parents are clueless. They think they know more about what adults can and should experience than their parents. Their vocabulary, their thoughts, their arguments sound so adult. Their minds are filled with images from the media, adult images, adult behavior—both violent and sexual—and their expectations for a materialistic lifestyle are high. The images of adult freedom and fun have been impressed on their minds and souls from a multitude of quarters, from TV, movies, and their friends. But one thing all the kids I see do not possess is the emotional maturity to use that freedom responsibly. They want desperately to act like adults, to experience adult feelings and privileges, but every single young person whom I have counseled lacked an understanding of how to manage how they felt. Kids are overwhelmed with adult images and try to act on adult impressions, yet behave like children— irresponsible, impulsive, and often irrational. This is what I call the New Adolescent, savvy but insecure. Appearing sophisticated but angry and resentful inside. Gifted but depressed. They can text message around the world, but cannot control their impulses to guzzle five beers in a row or to smoke marijuana to relieve their anxieties.

Addictive behavior continues to spiral out of control in our society, and the lifestyle of young celebrities continue to play out in our tabloids and on our TVs as some kind of empty validation of what parents see at home. It lulls them into the sense this must be the everyday experience of all adolescents. It is not. The good news is that the majority of teens are not contentious, unpleasant, heartless creatures who hate their parents and cannot self-manage their lives.

If we cannot trust the media for the images of what's normal, then where do we turn? Is there such a thing as a "normal adolescent?"

What is a Normal Adolescent?

The nature of adolescence has not changed in hundreds, maybe thousands of years, the teenage years are still a time of testing oneself, of challenging authority on its credibility, experiencing oneself sexually, emotionally, cognitively, and spiritually. It is a time of great risk and vulnerability. These are some of the reasons that adolescence can be turbulent. If a teen does not go through some difficulty and their parents experience some frustration, something is wrong.

The primary tasks of every adolescent are two-fold: separation and identification. It is during this time in their lives kids grow away from dependence upon their parents for everything including their views and opinions of the world, and into autonomous individuals with their own opinions, views, and who are engaged in their unique interests. It is normal during this time for them to push parents away, to test the limits, and to experiment. The adjustment is shocking to most parents. Just a year before the same kids who cherished their parents' opinions and presence are now embarrassed to have them around. This is normal. But what does a normal adolescent, from a healthy psychological point of view, look like? If you saw one, would you recognize him or her?

Too many times in our affluent society we think normal means possessing and accomplishing. Good grades, athletic accomplishments, a brilliant social circle, good looks, and high SAT scores are considered the core of what a normal or "outstanding" teenager looks like. While all of these things are good, in themselves they do not tell us much about a child's psychological health. Some of the most miserable people in the world are wealthy and powerful. According to psychologist Madeline Levine, "from a psychologist's point of view, outstanding children are those who have developed a 'self' that is authentic, capable, loving, creative, in control of itself, and moral."[6]

My term for the child's authentic self is "Lifespark." This is the adolescent's spirit, which includes beliefs, motivation, hopes, and dreams. Children who possess a healthy Lifespark are enthusiastic and internally motivated. Finding their Lifespark is the main task of the adolescent experience. When your son connects with his, you will know it. When your daughter finds hers, you will know she is on her way to adulthood.

Look carefully at these elements of a normal well-adjusted adolescent, they are self-motivated, self-regulating, loving, capable, moral, and enthusiastic about their lives. But you say "this doesn't describe any teens I know, particularly mine." You are right to a degree, because this is what they will grow into even though it is not what your son or daughter looks like today. Maturing is a process. This process of finding their Lifespark takes time, and sometimes it is messy and unpredictable. Children whose parents offer healthy parental support through this period of maturity by helping their adolescent find their Lifespark will become successful adults. So the question is what is normal during this chaotic process of growing up?

Separation from Parents

The one constant in children's development and the number one unconscious task of a teenager is to separate from their parents. A child has to go through the process of developing their own ideas of the world, about how it works, and where they fit into it. They can only do this if they separate from their parents. This happens on many levels: physically, emotionally, cognitively, and financially. Teens usually cannot separate from parents spiritually.

Teens have an overwhelming need to be independent, yet they lack the experience, emotional maturity, and financial ability to be self-sufficient. Nevertheless, the frustration of wanting to be independent remains and they will find a way to express it. This behavior is often called "acting out." It is natural for teenagers to do this and if your teen does not "act out" somewhat, this in itself may be reason for concern. However, there are safe ways to "act out" and there are unsafe ways. Distinguishing between the two will tell you if you have a kid who needs help or one who needs some space from parental involvement. Recognize that this separation from parental authority is the first step for them in forming their own identity.

Ways of Separating from Parents

Rebellion

Rebellion is a form of separation and in its most benign state could be seen as simply not adhering to the house rules, letting dirty clothes pile up on the bedroom floor, pushing for a later curfew, and general disagreements over household chores. These are typical and normal. A few decades ago the length of a boy's hair or the hems of a girl's skirt were key issues behind some spirited family disagreements. Today it may be the color of your child's hair, whether or not to allow nose rings, or the size and placement of a tattoo.

Rebellion driven by unresolved resentments is at the other end of the spectrum and can lead to serious issues if the underlying reasons are not resolved. Some other safe ways of rebelling that can produce conflict in the home and a more self-conscious form of expression include experimenting with hairstyles and make-up, listening to their own music, dressing uniquely—particularly to match their peer group—and wearing distinctive jewelry.

Arguing

Expressing their opinions, even argumentatively, is a form of cognitive separation. They are showing parents they can think for themselves and are beginning the intellectual steps to forming their own opinions, values, and worldviews. Disagreeing is a safe way for an adolescent to "act out." It accelerates the separation principle that drives all adolescent behavior and allows them to voice their own ideas, no matter how illogical they are. Teens will argue about most anything including concepts as an exercise in independence. One of the cognitive changes taking place during mid to late adolescence is a child's inability to see others' points-of-view. This can accelerate arguing, particularly with parents they may now disagree with.

Yet, arguing in itself is good. It shows cognitively everything is working. Kids are working through what they believe and what they know of the world. There is no need for parents to become alarmed unless it becomes excessive and ultimately disruptive, threatening to take over everything.

Anger

Anger alone is an emotion. There is no behavior attached to it. Many times teens' anger is more frustration with being stuck between childhood and adulthood. If they had the resources and capabilities to leave, they would—but they can't. Anger is not right nor wrong, good nor bad. It just is.

Cell Phone and Computer Addiction

Part of the normal process of becoming an individual is communicating outside the home with the peer group. Technology has changed the manner in which kids reach outside to their friends and to the world. The cell phone has made communication instant and easy, but the Internet has brought the world to our children's doorstep in unprecedented ways. Parents have to be particularly aware of their children's vulnerability to predators and other inappropriate material on line. The social sites, such as MySpace and FaceBook, are not inherently harmless. Parents must be able to keep-up with the current technology in order to monitor their children's access to the Internet.

If you as a parent are technically challenged, it is important to learn all that you can about the Internet, including MySpace, FaceBook, iPods and any other technology that is replacing you as the parent in this day and age. Technology will continue to become a more influential part of your adolescent's life and no parent can afford to ignore it.

Peer Acceptance

Kids separate from their parents for the purpose of forming their own unique identity. But they don't stay isolated from all relationships. When teens isolate themselves from all relationships, this can be a dangerous behavior. However, teens separate from parents, emotionally and cognitively, by becoming involved in a peer group. This gives them a whole new set of relationships with which to interact, to test their ideas, and to help define their interests and abilities. These relationships are often characterized by loyalty and trust. With their peers, teens learn to work through difficulties and observe how others in their group cope with common challenges. There is no doubt the peer group can have a positive effect in your child's life, just as it can have an equally negative one if your child is involved with the wrong group. Parents should not overreact or see it as a form of rejection that their children want to spend more time with their peers than with them.

How do I Know What's Normal Adolescent Behavior?

By now we've established that separating behavior is typical and normal, and the behaviors we talked about were general. Take some time and do an assessment of your child's behavior using the questions below. Take a piece of paper, if necessary, and jot down some notes.

- Are they doing well in school?

- Do they get along well in the family?

- Do they follow through on most agreements at home?

- Are their friends trustworthy?

- Do they obey most rules at home?

- Do you feel they are safe and not in any danger?

If a parent has a concern about any one of these questions, they should investigate their concerns with their children, but refrain from interrogating them. Each negative answer to any of the questions above could pose a serious problem for your teen.

Self-Destructive Behaviors

There are behaviors that clearly signal teens are having difficulty in the separation and individuation process. If you see any of the signs below, it is time to start asking yourself more questions regarding why your child is acting out self-destructively.

Are they at all

- Physically or verbally abusive?

- Running away?

- Hanging with the "wrong crowd?"

- Stealing?

- Damaging property?

- Refusing to cooperate?

- Truant or suspended from school?

- Maintaining unacceptable grades?

- Involved in alcohol or drug use?

- Fired from work?

- Having run-ins with the law?

- Involved in auto accidents or tickets?

- Involved in any gang activity?

- Threatening to harm themselves or others?—If so, immediate action should be taken

Assessing Your Teen

If you have any concerns about your teen's behavior, it is time to hone in on the problem and implement a remedy. Turn now to Appendix One-Assessment Guide and take some time going through each assessment to get a clearer description of your child's problem. Whether your child is an adolescent or midolescent, these assessments can help you. Once you understand the source, the solution will become more clear.

When is the time to seek professional help for your child? The more you identify any of these traits in your child, the more deeply she is in trouble. The time to get help is now!

Is there such a thing as normal?

Every family has challenges and difficulties. There is no easy way out of the adolescent experience except to get through it. Yet, just as there are unhealthy ways to respond to life there are also healthy ways, ones that engender emotional growth and maturity in our children. And these can be learned. In order for a parent to begin incorporating healthy ways of communicating, it's important to understand why and how they work. Let's take a closer look at these mechanisms.

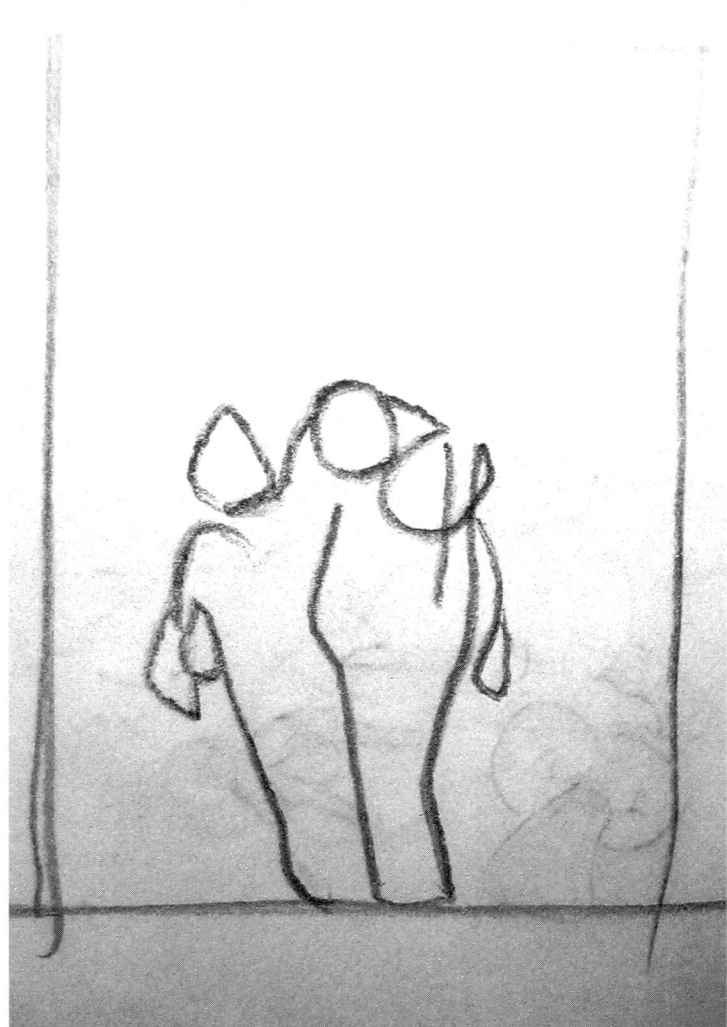

Chapter Three

Dynamics of the Healthy Family

It was 3:30 in the afternoon when Evan slammed the door to the kitchen, dropped his books on the counter and told his mother angrily he didn't intend to go back to school tomorrow, or ever, for that matter. Michelle was working on her computer responding to e-mails for her home business. She closed down her computer as he stomped up the stairs. It was obvious he was angry, but it could be about anything—a teacher, a friend, his girlfriend. She gave him a few minutes to settle down, then went upstairs and knocked on his door.

"Go away," he said.

"It sounds like you're angry," Michelle said. She knew from experience that if she started by asking him what happened she would be setting them both up for an argument. But by starting with identifying his dominant feeling, one of the Six Basic Feelings (mad-sad- glad-afraid-ashamed-hurt), she could help him express himself and process it.

"I ain't going to school ever again," Evan said.

Michelle resisted the urge to get into an argument or to try to resolve the problem before he processed his feelings. She stuck to what she knew worked best. "It sounds like you're angry. Let's talk about it."

"You don't know anything," his voice still rising. "I'm not angry."

Still talking through the door, she asked "Well, you slammed the door, then you stomped up the stairs and from the tone of your voice you sound mad."

Evan shuffled to the door, opening it slowly, letting her come in. He slumped back on the bed, face down in his pillow, behaving as if his whole world had caved in on him in one day. Michelle waited for him to talk.

"Gail broke up with me today."

She sat down on the edge of the bed, "Oh, honey. That must really hurt."

"No kidding," he said, sarcastically. "And she did it right in front of all her friends."

She knew if she asked for details at this crucial moment it would hinder the processing that was going on right now in his thoughts. She and Bob, her husband, had long ago given up the idea that they needed to have all the answers to their children's problems. Rather they learned that the best way to communicate and support their kids was to focus on helping them express their emotions in a non-judgmental environment.

"It sounds like you're feeling hurt right now because of Gail's words," she said, reflecting his feelings back to him.

"She broke up with me right at her locker in front of all her cheerleader friends."

Michelle could relate to his hurt, remembering back to her first breakup in high school. She sensed he was thinking that his social life was ruined and he'd never get another date. If there was one thing she knew from her own adolescence and from their two teens, life seemed entirely too dramatic at times.

It wasn't too much longer before Evan sat up and told her the details of what had happened. By dinnertime he was already talking about his homework that needed to be done for tomorrow. The pain hadn't completely passed, but Evan was well on his way in processing it. He would still have to deal with his friends at school. Michelle refrained from offering any solutions. She knew that the biggest part of growing up into a mature adult was for Evan to learn to solve his own problems. If he needed guidance, he would ask. By bedtime, he had regained some perspective and his world had come back into balance.

* * *

Healthy families do not consist of perfect people, but are led by parents who understand the importance of a healthy emotional life to themselves and to their children. A healthy family nurtures the Lifespark in each child, allowing them to grow emotionally by creating an environment of cooperation. Healthy family dynamics build a safe sanctuary in a world full of terror, a home where family members can express their deepest feelings in a non-judgmental environment free of consequences.

Even as I write this, I know there are those who have bad memories of feelings being expressed in damaging ways. You have probably witnessed rage, depression, violent acts, family betrayal, or you may have expressed them yourself. You have learned through experience that expressing feelings are bad, even shameful, and it is best to keep them to yourself. But feelings, such as mad-sad-glad-afraid-ashamed-hurt, were meant to be felt, then processed—but not always acted upon. We are designed with feelings/emotions as a means to monitor our environment. Learning to express our feelings in acceptable ways not only validates that we understand what we are experiencing, but teaches us self-regulation and leads to understanding our authentic selves.

In the healthy family, parents set-up acceptable boundaries, as Michelle did when she nurtured her son Evan's Lifespark. She taught her son it was okay to feel hurt and angry. A healthy person will acknowledge how he feels. He knows it is wrong to act on that hurt in vindictive and immature ways. But by allowing Evan the time and space to process his pain, there was no need for him to act out of his hurt feelings.

Michelle and her husband recognize the relationship between feelings and behavior. They have set up clear boundaries so their kids know what acceptable behavior is. Boundaries protect children physically, emotionally, and spiritually, and it is behind this security fence that is set up around the home where their children's Lifespark is nurtured. This allows room for the processing and validation of their authentic feelings. Feelings are meant to be felt, to be processed, and to be validated. They are a signal for us to sense our environment but not necessarily to react. In themselves, they are neither good nor bad. They are just the way a person feels at the moment as a result of something that was said or done.

In the course of treating patients over the last thirty years, I have found it worthwhile to simplify how we describe our inner states. By narrowing down the variety of internal responses to the Six Basic Feelings, I have found it easier for my clients to understand and articulate what they are feeling. We will continually refer to these Six Basic Feelings as we move deeper into the Art of Feeling.

One of the greatest gifts a parent can give to their children is to teach them the proper place and value of their feelings. You can do this by teaching them to identify the Six Basic Feelings that run through all of our lives in varying degrees: mad-sad-glad-afraid-ashamed-hurt. Memorize them; learn to identify them in yourself as you react to situations in your day. I am going to teach you to handle them with great skill in order to help you through the struggles of keeping your child sober, clean, and honest.

Validating your children's feelings and teaching them how to process them without acting out dangerously is critical to nurturing and protecting their Lifespark. This is the primary role of a healthy family and it is what David and Phyllis York, co-founders of "Tough Love" parent support groups, point to when they say one of the signs of a healthy family is that it is focused on "cooperation and not togetherness." Families who want to nurture the fantasy of always having a warming cozy feeling for each other are working on an illusion of togetherness. The reality is that the most parents can expect from adolescents who are working to forge their own identity is cooperation with each other. Cooperation is a mutual experience, modeled by parents who are willing to take a step back when their kids have an emotional reaction they do not expect or understand. Healthy parents understand that their kids are going to react to the events in their lives along a continuum of emotional responses, from the extreme to the benign. Parents who are able to support them through this process by actively listening will help them avoid damage to their Lifespark by assisting them to develop the inner skills they need to handle their emotional responses to life. By taking a step back, reflecting their emotions back to them, resisting the urge to react, and instead listening to how their kids are feeling, parents teach their children to process their feelings. Here, cooperation is fostered.

Because kids have an insatiable drive to become independent adults, they must pull away from their parents. It is to be expected that they will perceive the events and relationships in their lives differently than their parents do. At the heart of this difference is their Lifespark. Every child is born with all the elements of a healthy Lifespark that parents can either nurture or damage. Healthy families set up boundaries that allow room for growth and the nurturing of each child's Lifespark; in turn, a home with ill-defined or weak boundaries will produce kids with a damaged Lifespark.

What are Healthy Boundaries?

Children are born without boundaries. They learn them in the family system. Personal boundaries are necessary for survival in the world. Without healthy boundaries, kids have no ability to keep their Lifespark alive and burning bright. Proper boundaries keep toxic-shame from damaging aspects of the Lifespark and paving the ground for addictions in order to fill the vacuum in their lives. Boundaries protect a child's feelings, thoughts, and spirit, leaving them with a robust enthusiasm for life. They also protect one physically and sexually.

We learn our boundaries from our major caregivers (people who are older than us when we're children and who have great influence on us). These caregivers may be, but are not always, parents. They can be siblings, teachers, baby-sitters, extended family, stepparents, etc.

Boundaries are formed by what the major caregivers say, don't say, do, and don't do. Boundaries are essential for protecting the child's innate Lifespark. When boundaries are broken, the child's Lifespark is damaged and he is unable to respect others' boundaries. Boundaries exist in three main areas: physical, sexual, and emotional.

Physical boundaries help us determine when, where, how, and who we are willing to allow to touch us—essentially, how close we will allow others to come to us.

Sexual boundaries allow us to determine with whom, where, when, and how we will be sexual.

Emotional boundaries help us determine what we feel, and how we will respond to another person's behavior.

All of these boundaries are learned in the family of origin through an ongoing process that is constant and automatic. Everyone leaves their family of origin with a set of boundaries. Whether they are healthy or unhealthy is another question. When children are neglected or abused their boundaries become damaged and are not in tact. They generally will allow abusive or abandoning people in their lives until their boundaries are reset through participation in some kind of recovery program. People with healthy boundaries, who have learned them in a healthy family environment, won't allow abusive people to stay in their lives and are less susceptible to the pressures of the peer group, as well as to sexual and emotional manipulation. Much is at risk for children if they are not taught how to have healthy boundaries. Children without well-placed boundaries are susceptible to manipulation from outside forces that are usually not good for them. Peer pressure can overwhelm them, pressure to take drugs and drink becomes too strong to resist. It is difficult for them to discern when they are being sexually and emotionally manipulated. They will tolerate physical and emotional abuse.

Above all, boundaries are designed to protect the Lifespark, the innate set of qualities that each child is born with that must be nurtured and developed in order for the child to progress emotionally and spiritually into a productive and fulfilling adulthood.

What is a Lifespark?

The Lifespark is a set of natural qualities that exist in every person from birth. These qualities are seen in a pre-adolescent and adolescent as an enthusiasm for life that motivates them to grow and develop. Every child is born with these qualities and in the healthy family they are nurtured through healthy boundaries until the Lifespark glows bright in the child's life. A healthy Lifespark produces a self-motivated child. These qualities also characterize a healthy family.

There are Nine Qualities of a Lifespark:

Vulnerability: The family atmosphere allows each other to be vulnerable. Family members can argue, disagree, and are allowed to express differing viewpoints without hateful and demeaning language. No one is judged for how they feel. Feelings are not interpreted as thoughts or ideas and therefore not judged as such. Home is a safe place for children and their parents.

Imperfection: Children are allowed to be imperfect. They are not shamed for making mistakes and are not exposed to rigid rules and expectations. They are not expected to be perfect. A healthy family allows for imperfection and embraces and supports the other members when mistakes are made.

Immature: Family members are not expected to have all the answers. They are allowed to let down their guard at home and be child-like from time to time.

Worthiness: Healthy families exude and model attitudes of worthiness. They treat each other respectfully, and in instances when they fail to do so, they admit it and apologize for undermining one's sense-of-self-worth.

Spontaneous: Healthy families allow for spontaneity. They are not governed by lengthy pre-planned vacations or other events. They leave room for each member (young and old) to contribute to changing plans, ideas, or acting on the spur of the moment.

Curiosity: You never hear "curiosity killed the cat" in a healthy family. Their very foundation is based on learning and embracing new things. They encourage each other to take reasonable emotional risks.

Dependent: Healthy families are interdependent, rather than codependent upon one another. They trust one another and count on each other to protect the family unit. Family members do not feel an obligation out of guilt or shame to be loyal to one another. Rather they are proud and privileged to be part of the family.

Needy: It's okay that all family members occasionally become needy in a healthy family system. Needs are acknowledged and the family looks for ways to meet them as opposed to exposing one's vulnerability to the outside world. To do so is to create a shame base at the very foundation of the family.

Valuable: Each member of a healthy family believes they have value and their contributions (regardless of size) are acknowledged and validated as important. Healthy families don't use language that devalues other family members.

All of these are reasons why it is vital for healthy families to nurture the Lifespark until it burns bright in each family member. When it starts to dim, they gather around and figure out how to keep it burning bright.

In a nurturing family

- People will feel free to talk about their inner feelings.
- All feelings are okay.
- The person is more important than the performance.
- All subjects are open to discussion.

- Individual differences are accepted.
- Each person is responsible for his/her own actions.
- Respectful criticism is offered along with appropriate consequences.
- There are few "shoulds."
- There are clear, flexible rules.
- The atmosphere is relaxed.
- There is joy.
- Family members face up to and work through stress.
- People have energy.
- People express love to one another.
- Growth is celebrated.
- People have high self-worth.
- There is strong parental coalition.

While these are the ways that healthy families work there are also ways the family can damage the Lifespark. One of the most common is silence. When no one talks about the illnesses in the family, the alcoholism, when no one acknowledges the abuse in the family, when sadness is covered up and treated as an emotion to be ashamed of, children learn their feelings do not matter. And if their feelings do not matter, they quickly figure out they themselves must not matter. Whatever they are feeling must be as a result of their own inadequacies and defects. Toxic feelings begin to form, and these self-perceptions of worthlessness fester until they have fermented into full-blown toxic-shame. The Lifespark becomes damaged and the child begins to internalize toxic-shame as a dominant feeling. As Bradshaw points out, toxic-shame is at the root of all addictions.

Gwen was thirteen when she first ran away. When her mother finally brought her home she was furious at her daughter for putting her through all the worry. Her mom not only put her on restriction, but she took her cell phone, her computer, and her IPod away. A few days later after school, Gwen began arguing with her mother and after an intense verbal battle, broke down crying. For the first time she opened up and told her mother what was making her so angry. Several years ago, Gwen said her uncle Bill molested her when she stayed over night while her mom and dad were on vacation.

Gwen's mom was horrified. This was her favorite brother. Gwen's accusations couldn't be true and she told her daughter as much. Gwen's sense of shame collided with her anger at her mother's lack of interest in her. She sunk into a deeper depression as her anger at her mother ran head on into her shameful sense that "there must be something wrong with me" and pushed her into a deeper depression.

Gwen's Lifespark had suffered years of damage before she admitted to her mother about her molestation. It was this early damage to her sense of worth and her vulnerability that prevented her from talking honestly and openly with her parents. The toxic feelings about herself festered like an open wound, leading to unresolved anger. A shame-driven conscience drove her to act out, and ultimately to run away. However, when her mother devalued her daughter's moment of frank and open communication, she further destroyed Gwen's Lifespark, sending her into a tailspin of depression and eventually into drug abuse.

Gwen's mother further damaged her Lifespark by attacking her sense of vulnerability, of value, and her sense of worth. A shopworn adage often bantered about by those trying to help friends in pain is that "time heals all wounds." While it is true that the conscious pain, the rawness that is fresh in our minds and that saps our emotional strength, may diminish over time, the deep consequences of repeated damage to one's Lifespark does not heal itself. The damage, internalized as toxic-shame, the sense that a person is defective, mistake prone, and worthless, colors a person's emotional life with unconscious but repetitive patterns. This sense of defectiveness is internalized as toxic-shame. Again, as Bradshaw has pointed out, toxic-shame is the basis for all addictions. It is silent, undetectable from the outside. It often masquerades as something other than what it is, presenting itself as an addiction: alcoholism, sexual fantasies, workaholism, perfectionism, obsessive compulsive behaviors, and more.

From the outside, everyone who knows Gwen wonders why such a pretty, intelligent girl from a good and successful family finds her way into drug and alcohol addiction. But she has been set-up for a hard life until the pain becomes so great she is forced to seek a remedy and do the work necessary to find emotional healing. The good news is that it is possible for Gwen to find healing for her Lifespark. Anyone willing to do the work will find the solution.

Unresolved feelings do not go away. They burrow underground into whatever remains of the Lifespark, creating further damage. We do not stop feeling as human beings; rather we find ways of releasing those feelings. Emotions are a powerful part of our makeup. John Bradshaw calls them "e-motions or energy in motion."[8] They are the power behind our behavior.

When I was seven years old, I was playing out in front of my house with my Tonka trucks after a heavy rainstorm, making a little city in the mud. I built roads, bridges, quite an elaborate mud city that I was very proud of. I was convinced it was a masterpiece worthy of acknowledgement, particularly by my mother.

When my mother came out the door to call me for dinner, I was covered in mud. Looking me over only the way a mother can, she could have nurtured my sense of worth, my curiosity, and my spontaneous nature by admiring my handiwork. This would validate my Lifespark and help me internalize positive worthiness about myself. That inner sense that what I did mattered to her. This would eventually lead to establishing my sense of worth and competence as an adult.

When she came out the door, she looked me up and down and frowned until she saw the intricate pattern of roads, houses, bridges, and buildings I had built in the mud of the front yard. It was a critical moment for nurturing my Lifespark. It never occurred to me that I had torn up a section of the front yard lawn she so admired. She could have said: "What a builder you are! Now it's time to clean up and come in for dinner."

Instead she reacted and criticized me. Coming out of the house, she screamed at me, "Oh, my god, look what you've done to the lawn! Clean up this mess right now." She could not see my creativity and industriousness at work, my budding Lifespark. She only saw the damage I had done to her lawn.

This was the beginning of the damaging process of destroying my natural curiosity, my willingness to be vulnerable, and my ability to be imperfect in front of the family. As a result of many years of this kind of interaction with my mother, I became a people pleaser, always searching for people and situations that would give me the validation I craved. This led to many years of alcoholism and eventually into therapy where I learned how to get healing for my Lifespark. Criticism that attacks a child's personhood as opposed to his behavior is a corrosive acid to their Lifespark. Once a child's sense of vulnerability is damaged, he has a difficult time trusting others. Constant criticism, negative remarks, and disparaging statements concerning a child's attempts to feel like he matters to his parents damage all aspects of the Lifespark.

My mother's attack, though unwitting, on my personhood—my Lifespark—my curiosity, my vulnerability, my sense of not having to be perfect, my spontaneity and my freedom to be immature led me into many years of perceiving myself as defective. The driving sense that there was something wrong with me as a person, what I now know was toxic-shame, dominated my personality until I became an alcoholic. As a seven year old, there was no way I could have been aware how much a well-groomed front lawn meant to my mother, or that it was so important to her to be seen by her neighbors as a solid citizen. But I did intuitively feel that something else mattered to her more than my budding sense of self.

Damage like this can be undone. It is repairable, but it is a process. I will teach it to you as we go along.

Tips for Nurturing a Child's Lifespark

- Have clear family boundaries—physical, sexual and emotional—free from abuse and aggressive actions.

- Create an environment that is safe for children to express themselves emotionally. If it's okay for you to express your feelings openly and without consequence, it gives your child permission to do so.

- Learn to identify in yourself and other family members the Six Basic Feelings: mad-sad-glad-afraid-ashamed-hurt. Utilizing these labels will make your life much easier.

- Learn to reflect back to your children their feelings states, i.e., "it sounds like you are sad." Avoid making specific statements when guessing at one's feeling state. And, avoid asking questions. Questions put people on the defense, particularly when they are in the process of dealing with their feelings.

- Practice making statements that evoke emotion without soliciting anger. For example, "When I feel hurt I usually say things I regret the next day." Here the person can respond to your experience without becoming angry because you are not putting him in a defensive position. Also, by talking about your own experience you are less likely to evoke shame in the other person. Making a personal statement about how you deal with your own feelings is a natural way to open up a rational, healing discussion.

It is during the adolescent stage that the healthy Lifespark is nurtured by what parents or significant caregivers say or do, or don't say or don't do. This natural enthusiasm for life becomes internalized into a settled sense of self. At the core of the authentic *self* is a young adult who feels accepted and loved, that they matter to someone, and who possesses a growing sense-of-competence.

The ultimate goal for all healthy children is that as their *self* develops and it does so in tandem with their self-regulating habits and skills. Their choices are increasingly experienced as coming from within themselves, and the umbilical cord of parental control over choices and values is continually cut until it is completely severed. This self-motivation to love, to choose, to be a competent individual is at the heart of productive adulthood. The enthusiasm of the pre and early adolescent is transformed and internalized into a mature sense-of-self, one that is resilient and capable of functioning responsibly in the world. This is what a mature adult with an authentic *self* looks like.

But what happens when the authentic *self* is not properly internalized? What happens when in its place toxic-shame dominates a person's life? I believe this is at the heart of the midolescent crisis facing our nation. It is the lack of an authentic *self* that is the root cause of the emerging midolescent.

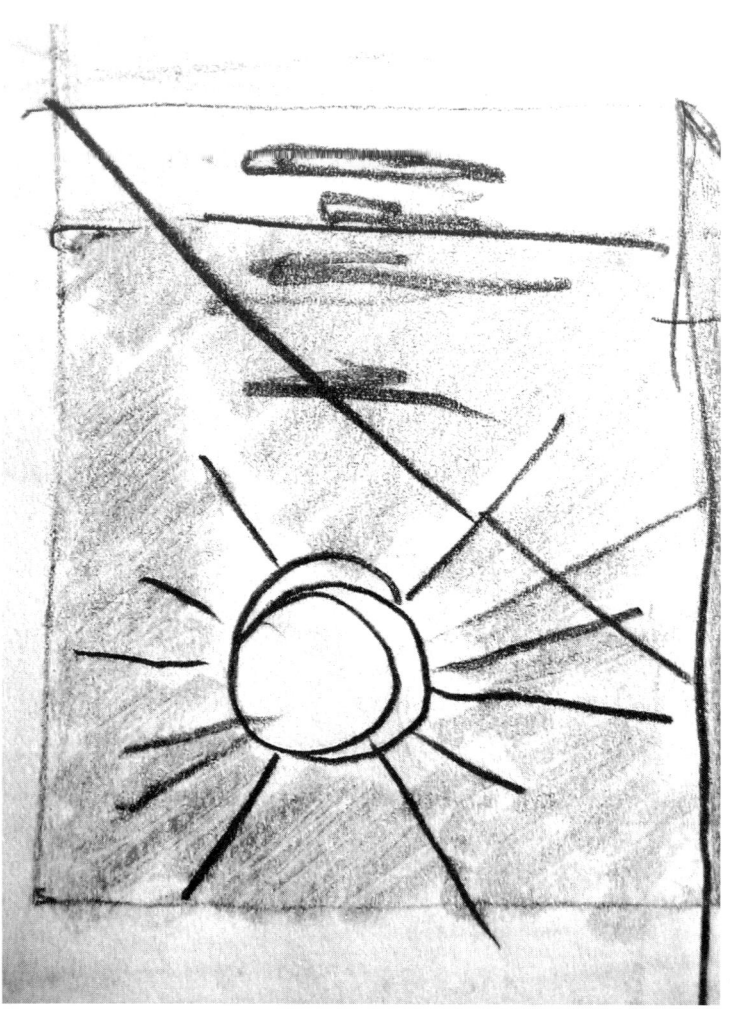

Chapter Four

Healing the Lifespark

By now you have probably figured out that a child who is stuck in the midolescent phase has failed to make the emotional leap into adult maturity. Parents often have difficulty admitting their child is stuck, many times tolerating disruptive or dysfunctional behavior to the point where there is no other alternative but to seek professional help. Since the midolescent's behaviors are tied directly to their lack of emotional development, they continue to display adolescent qualities: They are usually still living at home, but either don't contribute at all or contribute very little to the family household. Even though they don't pay rent, they help out very little around the house. They will stay out late and get angry when confronted about taking more responsibility in their lives. Since they have adult bodies and inclinations, they do not believe they should be told what to do. They are likely candidates for a wide variety of addiction problems: gambling, sex, Internet, drugs, food, smoking, or alcohol, to name some common ones. More importantly, they are probably addicted to their parents for their sense of self.

They are dependent on others to tell them what to do, what to feel, how to act, even what to think.

It is my experience that children who fail to make this leap do so primarily for emotional reasons. Yet when parents seek treatment for their child, and after assessments are completed, they often find their children suffering co-existing disorders. It is not uncommon for kids to have alcohol or drug addiction as well as a medical problem such as bipolar disease, anxiety, or depression. Substance abuse and addictions by nature are emotional; bipolar, anxiety, or schizophrenia are organic problems and are considered medical issues; psychological problems are typically thought disorders.

The approaches I am laying out in these pages are proven to help children mature emotionally. Yet if your child is suffering from substance abuse or other addictions, these conditions may co-exist with any psychological or medical issues to hinder your child from moving forward into adulthood. It is imperative to address addictions first. It is impossible to experience emotional healing while desensitized to feelings through drugs, alcohol, or any other addiction. Once the detox is complete the emotional issue and psychological and medical problems can be addressed simultaneously in non-shaming ways.

If you suspect your child has problems in addition to a lack of emotional development, it is vital you consult a physician or mental health practitioner for a full diagnosis. Below are some of the common psychological or medical disorders that will hinder a child from moving out of midolescence and into fully functioning adulthood.

Some Common Psychological and Medical Reasons for Midolescence

- Attachment Disorder – Resists affection on parental terms. Intense control battles.
- Anxiety Disorders – Panic Attacks, post traumatic stress, etc.
- Mood Disorder such as Depression – Deep sadness, loss, and inability to "snap out of it."
- Personality Disorders – Obsessive-compulsive, borderline, narcissistic, paranoia, etc.
- Adjustment Disorders – Maladaptive reaction to identifiable stressful event (divorce, death)

Medical Disorders

- ADHD and Learning Disabilities – Attention Deficit Hyperactivity Disorder – Unable to focus, poor impulse control, etc.

- Bi-Polar Disorders – Mood disorder characterized by manic or hyper episodes alternating with depressive episodes.

If you suspect your child suffers from any of these disorders or something other than emotional problems, it is recommended you consult a physician or mental health practitioner in addition to working the exercises in this book.

Who's Responsible?

One of the questions I'm often asked is who is responsible for the midolescent child? Was it something that the parent brought on themselves? The easy answer to that, and one I hope every parent reading this book takes to heart, is that it doesn't really matter anymore.

There could be hundreds of reasons as to why your adult-child may still be living at home. Some are healthy reasons others are not. Some of it may be your fault, some not. Some part is your doing; some part your child.

But there are a variety of reasons I would like to list. Some are healthy and good reasons why your child may never leave your home or at least be there for an extended period of time. The unhealthy ones are reasons you should do everything you can to help them leave.

A few healthy reasons your adult-child may still be living at live at home:

1. Your adult-child is a full-time student and is maintaining a good GPA.
2. Your adult-child has a legitimate physical, psychological, or psychiatric issue that prevents them from being self-sufficient.

3. You made previous arrangements with your adult-child that he/she has a certain amount of time to work, save money, and plan to move out, and your child is on track with the plan.

4. Your adult-child has volunteered as caregiver for a sick or disabled family member and must live at home to do it.

5. Your-adult child is actively pursuing school or employment and you have a written agreement as to when, where how and what will be accomplished and your adult-child is on target with the plan.

6. Your adult-child is recuperating from an illness and would be better off living at home right now for his own good, not yours.

A few unhealthy reasons your midolescent may still be living at home:

1. You somehow kept your child back from growing emotionally because you are unable to handle your own feelings, and now you midolescent somehow meets your emotional needs.

2. You kept your child between you and your partner for years in order to "buffer" a dysfunctional relationship and now your midolescent can't break this role and therefore stays home to keep the peace.

3. You are a midolescent in adult's clothing.

4. You abused your child and now can't set boundaries because of the guilt you carry.

5. You did everything for your child during childhood and adolescence and never allowed her to make and account for mistakes. You are now bound by a non-verbal contract in which your midolescent calls the shots at home. You are frozen in toxic shame whenever you attempt to "parent" this person.

6. You have reversed roles and have become the emotional child in the relationship.

7. Your spouse left you some time ago and you took over as super parent. Now your child owes you and there is a sense of obligation that your midolescent must live at home and tend to your unmet emotional-intimacy needs.

8. Your child is afraid to leave and you are even more afraid than he is.

9. You are a recovering (alcoholic, addict, gambler, sex addict, food addict, psychiatric patient, etc.) and you have never learned how to be a parent. You also never learned the skill of "letting go." Additionally, your midolescent needs to stay close and watch out for you.

10. One parent wants him out; the other wants him to stay. Your midolescent is stuck in a position of loyalty and you want him to choose a parent and he can't.

11. You are a single parent and need your midolescent to provide a sense of security for you in order that you don't experience certain feelings about your abandonment issues.

12. You think your child can't survive without you or vice-versa.

13. Pick your own reason(s).

Common Reasons Why Kids Fail to Make the Adulthood Leap Emotionally:

In previous chapters, I touched on some of the scenarios that take place to damage a child's Lifespark. We could fill this entire book describing the different ways a child's Lifespark can be damaged, but based on my treatment experience I have put together some common patterns that seem to repeat themselves.

Parental Enmeshment

Kids, particularly the older ones, may become the emotional husbands when the father of the family is emotionally or physically absent. A son will often take responsibility for mom emotionally. When mom cries, he comforts her. A daughter who is enmeshed may become daddy's little girl and doesn't want to disappoint him. Her entire self-esteem is wrapped up in what her father says, does, doesn't say, or doesn't do. There are a wide variety of enmeshment scenarios that prevent a child from separating emotionally, physically, intellectually, or financially from their parents. It is somehow communicated to the child that if she leaves home, the parent will not be able to survive without her. Subsequently, she puts her life on hold. She doesn't date, she doesn't prepare for her future through furthering her education; rather she submerges her life into her family's life. And all too often she will fall into some sort of addiction.

Any of these situations will hinder a child's emotional development and plunge them into midolescent existence.

Children of Divorced Parents

A child will stay home to try to become a catalyst for keeping a marriage together. She gets so involved emotionally in the marital problems of the parents that she does not grow emotionally. She may also develop a sense that she has custody of the parents.

Children of divorced parents can often also have loyalty issues. Loyalty is simply an intimate trust between parent and child. Loyalty issues arise when a child, due to the situation, is forced to back-up one of the parents. Like a boy who must choose to live with mother or father because of divorce, it is always a no-win choice for the child. The only semi-comfortable situation for the child is when both parents continue to support one another, particularly when they are not in each other's presence.

Otherwise, the child will likely feel toxic-shame for not choosing the other parent.

Another example is when a divorced or separated parent meets a new potential mate. Let's say mom takes on a new boyfriend. Without discussing their feelings (in advance of the child meeting the new friend), the child becomes a disruptive force within the new relationship. The child becomes particularly disruptive if he likes mom's new friend. This happens if the child sees himself as being disloyal to his father for liking mom's new boyfriend. The child may feel sad and ashamed about this. And if mom and dad fail to recognize their child's feelings or encourage him to talk about them openly, the child will bury his sadness and shame and it will turn toxic.

Unresolved Resentments

Unfinished business with one's parents usually shows-up in adults as unresolved resentments. Resentments are unresolved feelings, and not necessarily anger. When children experience damage to their Lifespark and the parents' communication skills are poor or under-developed, resentments grow and fester, paralyzing a child from moving forward with their lives. Emotions are an energy force in a person's life. And when they resolve themselves inward as resentments instead of outward in positive avenues, emotional development stops.

Toxic Fear

When children have an inability to take a risk they are generally paralyzed by toxic fear. Remember, fear is a healthy emotion. It protects us from the unknown. However, toxic fear is not so much an emotion as it is a debilitating thought process. For instance, my mother could not swim and she had a fear of water. She passed this toxic fear onto me by telling me things like "did you know you can drown from one raindrop." She reinforced this toxic fear in me with repetitive messages such as: "Don't go near the water, you could drown." "Never attempt to swim for at least an hour after you eat." Now my mom was simply trying to keep me safe. I believe her rationale for these terroristic messages was if she could keep me away from the water I couldn't possibly drown. In essence, my mother passed her own irrational fear of water onto me as a child in an effort to protect me. By the way, I cannot swim a stroke to this day. This is an example of a parent's skewed thinking and how it can evoke toxic fear into a child that will have lifelong effects. This works with all feelings in all situations. Therefore, one of our jobs as parents is to avoid sending toxic-emotional messages to our kids and when we do so, recognize and rectify it before our child ends up resenting us for it and living with us the rest of our lives. Emotional scare tactics set the stage for a child to become dependent on their caregivers to forever meet their financial, emotional, and physical needs.

Dysfunctional Parenting Styles

There are two major dysfunctional parenting styles that contribute to the damage of the Lifespark.

1. **The Authoritarian Parent:** this parent works by rules, intimidation, yelling, and uses fear as a motivator often accompanied by a crippling critical nature and negative communication style.

2. **The Permissive Parent:** A parent who is more concerned about being a friend to their children than effectively parenting them into adulthood. This will create warm-hearted children with no boundaries. A child with no boundaries will not develop any true sense of themselves, of who they uniquely are, and will be open to numerous unhealthy influences.

Parental Abandonment

Parents today are busy. More busy than ever before. Often they are too busy to spend time with their kids and when they do it is rushed, hurried, and not focused on the child's needs. It is possible for parent and child to live in the same house for many years but have little to no actual intimate communications. This damages the Lifespark because it attacks a child's sense of worthiness, the sense that they matter to someone significant in their lives. Abandonment can be emotional, physical, and spiritual because it attacks and damages a child's sense of worthiness.

Parental silence is a form of abandonment. When parents do not talk to their kids, the child is forced to make up their own journey in life. Lack of communication most likely will result in a family with no boundaries. Growing up in my own family, there were no stated rules. I did not discover I had done something wrong until I had broken one of the unspoken rules and then I suffered a consequence for it. That is how I learned the rules. Of course, the rules would change from time to time because they were based on my parents' emotional condition. I could come in one night at eight o'clock and be put on restriction. Two weeks later, I could come in at midnight and no one would say a word. Silence damages the healthy dependency needs of a child.

Faulty Communication

Negative critical comments about a child, their work, their person, their looks, their clothes, their abilities, or their efforts are extremely damaging. I am not talking about genuine feedback designed to help a child improve their skills or efforts, but words that attack a person's worthiness and leave them with the sense that they are in some way defective as a person.

These negative messages take many forms. Telling a child he will never amount to anything or questioning where he came up with such a stupid idea damages a child's vulnerability and willingness to be curious and try new ideas and new skills. Parents who insinuate a daughter cannot perform up to their expectation level in school, at hobbies, at sports, or anything she has an interest in can erode her sense of worthiness and willingness to be imperfect. This sets her up for an empty life of perfectionist tendencies. Of all the ways to damage a child's Lifespark, negativism and a critical approach have the most subtle but long-term consequences. They do not leave any outward bruises, but multiple areas of a child's Lifespark will feel attacked and suffer destruction inside. This cycle results in the child internalizing toxic-shame, which we have already described as a sense that the *self* is defective. This feeling is the root cause of all addictions and at the heart of the midolescent malaise.

Over involvement

Parents who won't give their children breathing space to grow tend to raise kids who are too fearful to leave the family nest. Kids need room to grow, to experiment, to fail, to be children, and to make some of their own decisions about their own likes and dislikes. Some parents are like personal helicopters, hovering over their child's life, managing all the trivial detail of daily decisions. These parents tend to produce kids with no self-confidence and no inner-motivation. Kids like this have a hard time cutting the umbilical cord. It is hard to say who is holding on tighter, the child or the parents who just won't let go.

Any of these elements will damage a child's Lifespark, hindering their emotional development and their growth into autonomous, authentic self-motivated adults. In the previous chapter, I discussed what constitutes a healthy Lifespark and described its qualities and components. Every child is born with these qualities intact. Let us now take a brief look at what happens to the Lifespark of a child when it is injured or damaged. Through any of the parental behaviors mentioned above, elements of the Lifespark that originally were positive have been turned into negative forces dominating a midolescent's life.

Components of our Lifespark

In the left column are the natural characteristics of one's Lifespark. All children naturally possess all of these characteristics. In the right column lies the characteristics of the Lifespark as a result of a pattern of neglect, abuse, or harm inflicted upon a person during their life. As children we all experience emotional damage; however, if an adult intervenes soon after the damage occurs, we will avoid long-term consequences to our natural Lifespark. Notice in the right column that damaged characteristics of the Lifespark result in the opposite experience as the healthy one.

CHARACTERISTICS OF THE LIFESPARK

Healthy / Natural Characteristics	Unhealthy/Damaged
Spontaneous	Suspicious
Worthy	Questions Self-Worth
Healthy Dependence	Co-Dependent
Immature/Childlike	Irresponsible/Childish
Imperfect	Perfectionist or Pessimistic
Vulnerable	Rigid/Closed
Curious	Apathetic/Uninterested
Needy	Needless or Insatiable
Valuable	Incompetent or Disrespectful

When a parent begins to understand what their child is experiencing and how they feel in the moment, the healing process can begin. A child does not become dysfunctional overnight, and their healing is not going to happen quickly, but it will happen. Typically it is poor communication skills between parent and child that underlie these problems. The next step in helping your child get unstuck is for you as a parent to get unstuck, to be able to express yourself at a feeling level by learning the Six Basic Feelings.

Healing the Lifespark

It is not unusual for kids transitioning out of family into emerging adulthood to have experienced some form of damage to their Lifespark. However, those who suffer significant emotional damage are unable to move forward with their lives and unfortunately fall into the treadmill existence of midolescence. Theirs is a nebulous life, directionless and full of turmoil. While their peers are out establishing careers, traveling, dating, discovering their strengths and passions, these kids are at home getting high or staying out until all hours of the morning just hanging out, or engaged in some repetitive addictive behavior that controls and ruins their lives.

In my experience, a midolescent's Lifespark can be healed by practicing the Art of Feeling I'm going to teach you. I have seen hundreds of kids respond to my counseling strategies and go on to lead productive adult lives.

Parents as Healers

First and foremost, a parent of a midolescent who wants to help their child grow up must learn to label their own feelings. Parents of children who have not learned healthy ways of expressing their feelings have to accept the truth that more than likely their children have learned their faulty communication habits from them. This statement is not meant to shame parents or to malign their family-of-origin. Quite to the contrary, it is meant to facilitate healing. Parenting skills are hereditary. They are passed down from generation to generation the way a mother passes on the family heirloom of her mother's wedding ring to her daughter—from mother to daughter to granddaughter. Communication skills become traditions, accepted ways of doing things, which become habits that are passed on in the same way—from father to son to grandson. Everyone's communication skills were learned in the schoolroom of the family.

If you understand that as a parent you are not at fault for the family you grew up in, you had no say in your choice of parents, you will also understand that you are not entirely at fault for the communication style you have used up to this point. This realization will allow for shame-free healing. Your parenting skill in terms of your inability to foster true intimacy with your child is probably limited. This is not entirely your fault. However, it is imperative to understand that it is your limited communication skills, particularly in the areas of communicating intimate feelings that have contributed to your child's midolescence. When you can accept that and have ruled out any medical or psychological problem for your child's inability to make the leap into adulthood, their problems in maturing stem directly from their inability to express their feelings in healthy productive ways. That is my experience and the basis of the healing therapy I am teaching here. This direct inability to communicate on a feeling level is something they learned from you, their parent, which you learned from your parents and so on.

With effort, determination, and some clear direction, you can learn new skills that will not only foster significant healing in your own life, but in the lives of your spouse and children. The skills I will teach you will help you in all areas of life including communication with co-workers, friends, and extended family.

Parents who heal become natural healers.

True intimacy is experienced when a person is able to express their feelings. For this reason, learning to use the Six Basic Feelings is vital to your emotional and psychological well-being. Many people spend their whole lives avoiding dealing with their feelings, while in most cases in the long run it is easiest to confront them. Avoiding your feelings is the number one reason people tend to lack an authentic sense-of-self. Emotionless kids in adult bodies tend to lead self-destructive lifestyles and have a life full of relationship difficulties.

The easiest way to learn to understand your own feelings is by using the following descriptive labels. I have found that narrowing it down to just Six Basic Feelings gives people the ability to easily remember, practice, and integrate the Art of Feeling into their lives.

The Six Basic Feelings:

Mad is our emotional response to not liking or agreeing with something. Its okay to dislike something and feeling MAD about it is appropriate. Acting out (arguing, throwing things, threatening others) are behaviors and not feelings and are therefore unhealthy and unproductive.

Sad is our emotional response to loss. Whether you lose your wallet, lose your way, or lose a friend or relative, loss is loss and the feeling of sadness is an appropriate and healthy response to loss.

Glad is an emotional response which encompasses all euphoric feelings. It's our response to having what we want, being comfortable, doing what we enjoy, and having freedom. It is also having emotional balance. Glad, like all other feelings, is a process, not a reward or destination.

Afraid (or fear) is our emotional response to the unknown or the distrusting of a person, place, or thing. When you feel afraid in a particular situation, it is because you sense danger or that something is wrong. Fear helps to keep us aware and safe.

Ashamed (or healthy shame) is our social feeling. Healthy shame is experienced as a mild embarrassment. It helps us to keep our behavior from overwhelming others. For example, if you make an offensive comment to another person and you have a healthy sense of shame, you should be able to sense their pain. Feeling ashamed at that point would be a healthy response. Your next step would be to apologize to that person for the comment. Following through with the apology is what gives you the healthy sense of shame, which contains your reaction and helps to prevent you from repeating the behavior again and again. People with no healthy sense of shame lack emotional boundaries.

Hurt is our emotional response when trust is violated. For example, if you walk into a restaurant and find your good friend is talking negatively about you behind your back, it is only natural you will feel hurt. You trusted this person with your personal information. Leaving at once would be a good idea. You can speak to your friend about it at another time. On the other hand, if you fly off the handle and yell at the person, this can be destructive and is not a healthy way to express your hurt. Again, the healthy response would be to walk away, contact your friend at a later time, and tell him, "Ben, you were talking about my private information to others behind my back at the restaurant. I feet hurt by what you did."

It is imperative to your healing to learn to always use one or more of the Six Basic Feelings when expressing yourself. When you label your feelings, you limit them. By limiting them, you will find it easier to understand what you are actually experiencing. The more words you use to describe your feelings, the more confused you will become. Confusion is the natural enemy of feelings.

First, memorize these Six Basic Feelings (mad-sad-glad-afraid-ashamed-hurt). Second, practice identifying them every day as you work, as you drive, as you talk with co-workers or friends. Become sensitive to the world of your own inner state. Keep the list of feelings at your desk, in your car, on your refrigerator, or anywhere you can access it easily. Are you mad? Are you glad? Are you feeling ashamed of something you said or did? Are you feeling hurt at a friend's or spouse's words? Acknowledge what you are feeling apart from any reaction. Write it down if possible. Include the person's name, the day, the time, and place. This will help you to debrief the feeling later while avoiding an embarrassing reaction.

Feeling Exercises

The following are two exercises you can practice to create a better awareness of your feeling states. The more aware you are of how you are feeling at any given moment the better you will understand yourself. The better you understand yourself, the stronger your boundaries and personal decisions will be. This is key to becoming a more effective communicator with greater intimacy.

Feelings Journal: Each night think of four significant parts of your day and try to express in writing (if you haven't already) what you were feeling in those moments. It's okay to guess. Be sure to use one or more of the Six Basic Feelings (mad-sad-glad-afraid-ashamed-hurt) and write down your dominant feeling in the journal. Do this for thirty days and you will see a pattern emerge of your dominant feelings. This is important because if you have a dominating feeling that you are failing to express to others, it will run your life and dictate your behavior.

Feelings Log: During waking hours, using the list of the Six Basic Feelings (mad-sad-glad-afraid-ashamed-hurt), every fifteen minutes jot down two ways you are feeling. Do this as often as you can throughout your day. You will begin to see a pattern.

More often than not the patterns that emerge are connected to specific situations. Are they the same situations? Are they different? Can you connect the dominant reactions to scripts from your past or situations with your parents or family life? Learning to identify how you feel in particular situations will help you understand how your child might be feeling in a given situation. Learning what is behind a particular or recurring feeling will give you insight into why one particular feeling seems to be dominant. This exercise will enhance your ability to communicate in ways you never imagined as we move along with the exercises.

Separating Feelings, Thoughts and Behaviors

The next step is to learn to separate three things we experience on a daily basis. The healing process begins when we can quickly and effectively understand the difference between our feelings, our thoughts, and our behaviors. More than likely your midolescent child suffers from a confusion of these three because you as a parent do. Remember, you learned your parenting communication style from your parents, and your kids learned their patterns from you.

Learning to separate feelings, thoughts, and behaviors will become the foundation for healing and healthy communications.

Feelings: The six described above (mad-sad-glad-ashamed-afraid-hurt). When expressing a feeling, such as anger, sadness, or fear, the operative idea is that the statement is short. "I feel angry," is an expression of feelings. Feelings are about your inner state, and when you narrow it down to just six, it is easier to describe what you are feeling: (mad-sad-glad-ashamed-afraid-hurt). Memorize these descriptions and practice identifying how you feel. One truth about feelings is that they are never right or wrong. They just are.

For example: "John, yesterday you lied to me about the money you owe me. I feel hurt." Hurt is how you felt yesterday and is also how you feel right now because you haven't resolved it yet. Hence, the word "feel" is used as opposed to "felt" which represents past tense. Always use the word "feel," because it means you are in the "here and now," which will get your feelings across to others. No one can argue or debate that you feel hurt by someone else's dishonesty. It is the way you are feeling at that moment.

Thoughts: "You lied to me," is a thought. All you have to do is put, "I think…" in front of it and you can easily recognize it as a thought. Thoughts are characterized by an evaluation, a judgment, a determination of guilt, innocence, or some form of value. A thought can be fact-based, but even then, thinking that is purely intellectual or supposedly objective can have a value judgment attached simply because the speaker is trying to prove someone or something right or wrong. When I say, "You have never been honest with me," I am expressing a value judgment in the form of a thought that can be debated, argued about, rebutted, rejoined, or proved wrong. Parents who lead conversations with their thoughts are setting themselves up for an argument. One they probably cannot win.

Behavior: These are the easiest to identify since it is always an action. Actions are at the opposite end of feelings. "I'm mad," is a feeling and is neutral. Feelings are neither right nor wrong. Throwing a chair across the room because you are feeling mad is a behavior that is wrong and one that will likely get you in trouble. Unresolved feelings such as anger and shame will work themselves out in a child's life via inappropriate behavior.

This may seem like a simple exercise, but behind its simplicity is your ability to communicate on a feeling level. Parents who cannot distinguish between a thought and a feeling will only communicate their thoughts because this is typically how we are trained. Not only will your emotional needs never be met if you cannot communicate your feelings, but you will never experience true intimacy with those you love the most.

It is human nature that when a person is judged, accused, made to experience guilt or toxic-shame they will not want to be vulnerable or in any way transparent about how they truly feel inside. Even when a person deserves to be judged, or announced guilty, communications stop when the judgments are pronounced against them. Kids who are continually spoken to in judgmental ways find they become cut off from themselves emotionally, lose their willingness, and eventually their ability, to communicate from their inner selves. When communication is based on thoughts laden with value judgments, particularly in the highly charged relationships typically found in parent-child relationships, communications cease. The child's willingness to be spontaneous, vulnerable, and childlike is damaged. All of this damage settles into children in different ways. Some get sullen, depressed, and withdrawn. Some become rebels and begin a pattern of destructive behavior. Some become so depressed they have a hard time functioning and participating in life. Almost all of them fall into some type of addictive behavior.

All of this can be healed to a great degree. Concerned parents who work on the exercises described in this chapter will have a foundation for communications that will produce intimacy with their child. I have never failed to see it happen. It takes some work, but it is well worth it—for them and for you.

Exercises: Your First Thirty (30) Days

Feelings Journal—Thirty (30) days (see description page 71)

Feelings Log—Three (3) days (see description page 71)

Chapter Five

Communicating Your Feelings

In this chapter, I'm going to teach you how to present your unresolved feelings, or what we at Chapman House refer to as your "resentments." These techniques are a critical part of your communication success with your child and with your spouse. For that matter, I believe you will find these skills are transferable to every aspect of your life: your work, your social network, as well as your extended family. They have the potential to make all of your relationships more productive and meaningful.

Now that you understand the difference between thoughts, feelings and behaviors, we can move on to the beginning exercises of effective communication. There is hope for relational healing if communications work on a more intimate level. Accomplishing this will not be easy since you are now entering an undiscovered territory in your relationship with your child, your spouse, and maybe even with yourself.

The process of communicating your feelings begins with presenting your resentments. There is a way to do this so that it does not produce a negative reaction in your child that usually results in nothing but denial and arguing. Remember, we already discussed in the last chapter that when you begin your conversations off with thoughts, they easily turn into accusations in the other person's mind. Thoughts, judgments, evaluations, and opinions can be argued over, discussed, and justified. Feelings simply exist in the one who feels them. And in that simple truth lays the power and purpose of leading all communications with your feelings. They open up lines of communications that other forms of expression typically shut down.

All too often parents want to strike out at their children verbally and prove their position—how they've been wronged, disrespected, and taken advantage of. All of that is probably true and more; however, by lashing out with accusations, you only solidify the wall of silence between you and your child. The failed communications will only be guaranteed to continue. You must consider the fact that the gulf of intimacy between you and your child or spouse that now exists has been created by poor communication skills. Give this process a chance. I believe The Art of Feeling will revolutionize your relationships in ways you never imagined.

The Process—Writing Twenty Resentments to Your Midolescent

Here is the chance to work on twenty resentments you have toward your midolescent child (this method can also be used with anyone important in your life such as your spouse, father, mother, sibling, or significant other.)

Resentments are unresolved feelings and in general, they are not all about anger. They can include any feelings that you have not resolved in your past, such as anger, sadness, fear, shame and/or hurt. When writing your list, always include one or more of these five of the Six Basic Feelings in each specific example: mad-sad-afraid-ashamed-hurt.

How to Write Your Resentments

Although resentments are unresolved past feelings, you may go as far back in your relationship with your midolescent as twenty years or as recently as two days; however, when you write out your narrative, use the present tense as if it is happening now. Additionally, be sure to focus your resentments on your midolescents behavior. Never attack their person.

How to Structure your Resentments

The structure of how you present your resentments is vital to your success. First, start with the name of the specific person you are addressing. Our name (Mary, Tom, etc.) or title (Mom or Dad) is our initial identity and verbalizing it gets the person's immediate attention. Second, describe the specific situation. Always focus on the behavior, never on the person. Focusing on the person is usually perceived as an attack. Third, state precisely how you feel in this situation. Do not use non-specific descriptors such as, "kind of"; "sort of"; "a lot"; "a little."

These, and words like them, make communications non-precise and give the person you are talking to the opportunity to discount what you are saying.

It is important to use this format because it prevents our natural tendency to want to justify our feelings. For instance, we typically will say, "You hurt my feelings when you didn't pick me up like you said you would." This statement seeks to blame the listener for the speaker's feelings and could create an argument. Either party in this budding argument could have misunderstood the directions to the pick-up point or the time. The possibilities are endless and so are the arguments. The goal is not to justify the speaker's feelings, to prove they are right or wrong, nor to demean the other person for their faulty judgment in not following through with showing up, but simply to express how the speaker feels.

Review of structure:

1. "Bobby" – (person's name or initial identity)

2. "Yesterday you were supposed to pick me up after school, but you didn't show up." (specific incident)

3. "I feel hurt." (State specific feeling, using an "I" statement so as not to blame the listener for your feeling.)

Notice how simple and straight forward this example is? Short and to the point is the most effective way to communicate emotions. Remember, one or more of the Six Basic Feelings. Mad-sad-glad-afraid-ashamed-hurt should always be the last word. This prevents us from continuing to do what we have been doing for years—defending or justifying our feelings to others. When we use a feeling word before we describe the specific incident, it tends to sound like we are backing-up the feeling. This creates doubt in the listener's mind and gives them room to argue about the nature of your feelings. If you always close your statement with a feeling word or words, trust me, there will be little arguing.

First Example:

This is an ineffective way of communicating feelings between mother and son:

"You're always screaming at me in front of other people, Tom. I'm pretty disgusted with you."

Although this statement may be true, Tom will never hear his mother's feelings for several reasons. First, she needed to lead with Tom's name in order to ensure gaining his attention. Next, she used the word "always." This will certainly lose Tom's attention because nobody "always" does anything. It will be justified in Tom's mind that mom doesn't know what she's talking about and therefore, her statement and feelings can be rejected or denied. Next, she failed to specify who the people were who witnessed Tom screaming (Mary, Greg, Mira, etc.). Naming witnesses brings evidence and credibility to the statement and ensures Tom's attention. Next, "I'm pretty disgusted with you" is a statement that if she hadn't lost Tom's attention or respect yet, she has now. First, the word "pretty" minimizes the feeling (that's if there had been a feeling at the end of the statement to begin with). She wasn't "pretty disgusted" she was disgusted! However, the word "disgusted" fails to describe her feelings in a way Tom can absorb. Finally, she ended her statement with the word "you." And, that's all that Tom will remember— he's to blame.

Can you see how a simple statement can be such a destructive force? This underlies the importance of structuring your statement before presenting it. Understandably, you will not sit down and structure every statement before speaking with your midolescent or significant other. However, if you practice this daily for a few weeks the process will come naturally. Only during very important conversations or situations will it become necessary for you to write out your thoughts and feelings before sitting down and presenting them. However, when you do this preparation in advance, you should always invite the other person to do the same. It is up to you to teach your family the Art of Feeling. This communication style will make talking about situations and feelings productive, not stormy and unproductive.

First example presented effectively:

"Tom, I resent it when you scream at me in front of other people. One example is when you screamed at me in front of Bill at Kim's birthday party. I feel ashamed and hurt."

Notice in this example Mom first stated Tom's name (initial identity), and that got his attention. Next, she presented her statement using an event (specific example), including the names of those present. This helps Tom to visualize and remember the specific situation. Finally, she closed with her feelings (present tense) and didn't blame Tom. She simply owned how she felt.

You can practice the Art of Feeling by mimicking this example; just take one feeling and situation at a time. Most of us want to express every feeling we have in order to get them off our chests. That simply doesn't work. We have to resolve our feelings one situation at a time. Once we master this technique, we will be able to resolve our feelings as they arise, thus minimizing building resentments toward others. The Art of Feeling will help to eliminate stress while building trust and intimacy within your family.

When a person is confronted with one specific situation at a time and the associated feelings, it minimizes their potential to become defensive. The speaker should always keep the statement in the present tense, because even though a feeling may be connected to a situation in the past, if the feeling remains unresolved it is sill affecting their life today.

Second Example:

This is another ineffective way of communicating feelings between mother and son:

"Why don't you start acting your age? Pushing people and embarrassing people in front of your family will never get you anywhere. You should be ashamed of yourself, Tom."

This statement would produce the same effect in the listener as if the speaker had poked him in the eye. It carries the same dysfunctional components as the first example only this one includes questions and shaming. Notice Mom started off with a question. Questions will always set Tom up to defend himself. He can't hear Mom because he's busy trying to answer the question. And, in answering the question, Tom becomes confused. How does one act their age? Mom's question and statement is shaming and only creates more distance between her and Tom. Further, Mom didn't even include herself in the statement and that's who she was supposedly expressing her feelings for. You must be in your own resentment. Finally, this was a lecture. A lecture coming from a parent who, in the child's mind, has little or no credibility will simply create more resentment. This example is completely counterproductive.

More effective way:

"Tom, I resent that you pushed me when we were at your grandmother's house the day she had a stroke. I feel mad, sad, and hurt."

Notice Mom used Tom's name to get his attention. Then her description focuses on one specific action. Tom may have exhibited a number of unacceptable behaviors that day, however, Mom wisely focused on one. It is easier to hear and handle one situation when communicated effectively. As I mentioned earlier, it's all too often we try to sum-up a whole host of irritating behaviors in one conversation. It is simply too difficult for anyone to internalize a wide range of feelings and incidents at one time. When people become overwhelmed with too many feelings from too many incidents, they will check out cognitively and begin to think about ways to exit the conversation. Finally, Mom closed by describing her feelings. This leaves Tom to ponder how his behavior impacted his mom's feelings.

When you first consider these techniques, you may think this is an exercise of splitting fine hairs because using these exact words cannot be that important. Yet, it is these very techniques that take into account what all the healing disciplines have come to acknowledge, that we live in our hearts (feelings), but we hide in our heads (thoughts). By forcing a child or a spouse to defend themselves intellectually, they will not be present in the conversation and will not engage emotionally. Communications will cease and feelings and situations will not get resolved.

The purpose of these exercises is to open up communications by resolving feelings and situations one at a time. It is not to prove you are right and your midolescent is wrong, but to create an open avenue so real intimacy can take place.

Mom's intent in the first scenario is to teach Tom something about his behavior. But instead, she creates doubt, suspicion, and distance; certainly not trust or intimacy. In the second scenario, Mom used his name, which gets his immediate attention. She then goes on to describe one specific event that he cannot deny because they were both there. She takes responsibility for her feelings and expresses them without blaming or shaming Tom. Since she expressed her feelings without being judgmental or threatening, she opens up communications between them. Just because Mom communicates her feelings, it doesn't mean he's going to immediately change. But since she demonstrates how to express her feelings in a healthy manner, she begins to give Tom a pattern to follow, a way for him to express himself without acting or striking out. It will take time, but if used consistently Tom will respond positively.

So what can Tom's mom expect by using this method? Is it reasonable to see Tom change overnight? If Mom was sharing her feelings with the idea to manipulate him in some way to get him to change then he would end up resenting her even more. But if she communicates in order to resolve her own emotions as well as the situation, she is teaching her son how to resolve his own emotions.

Behavior change comes naturally over a period of time as the result of trust and open communication. It took years of ineffective and counterproductive conversations to get to the place your family may be at today. However, by modeling a healthy expression of feelings, your children will have a positive model to follow.

Third Example:

This is an ineffective way of communicating feelings between father and son:

"You don't pick up anything around the house, you won't work, and you expect me to wait on you hand and foot. I feel you don't care about me or anyone else."

Did you catch the first problem here? Tom's father is not addressing him by name. Next, again he is mixing in too many situations and feelings. Tom would have a hard time sorting out what his father is actually trying to communicate. Tom's father is not specific and is setting up Tom to defend himself with an argument.

Dad's feeling statement is not about feelings at all: "I feel you don't care about me" is a thought, not a feeling.

If I had to guess at Dad's feeling here based on "I feel you don't care about me," I would say he feels hurt. Remember, hurt is about trust being violated and a family member not caring about another is a deep violation of trust. The last part about Tom not caring about "anyone else" could be viewed by him as Dad being out of control because he is grasping at unknown people who aren't even involved in this situation. Tom could reasonably think that Dad is the one that needs help. Based on this dysfunctional statement, this could be true. Dad needs to look at how he approaches Tom with his feelings because in this scenario, it appears that on the surface dad is angry. Yet if you understand the Art of Feeling it is obvious Dad feels hurt.

The above fails to foster communication; it cuts off effective intimacy and tends to create even more resentment.

More effective way:

"Tom, I resent it when you leave your clothes lying around for others to pick up. Just today you left your shoes, jacket, and undershirt on the living room floor. I feel hurt and mad."

Here dad addressed him directly, gaining his immediate attention. There is no trying to justify the feelings or to manipulate; it is just a statement of specific facts and a statement of how dad feels at the moment.

There is nothing to argue about or dispute because it is specific on all counts.

Practice

By writing out this exercise of twenty different incidents, you are going to hone your skills at presenting your feelings. When you are finished, read them verbatim into a voice recorder. Next, play back your resentments one at a time. Use the guide on the next page of this book to be sure all components of your resentments are present in your statement. Listen for inconsistencies, blaming, controlling, manipulations, or anything that would make you defensive or uncomfortable if you were on the receiving end of this statement. You could also find a reliable person to whom you could practice reading your statements. This should never be your children or even a close family member. It's just too difficult for a family member to be objective. Share this with a person who can be trusted to give you objective feedback. You should practice expressing your resentments until you have mastered your reactions. By learning to respond to a difficult situation and not reacting out of emotional pain, you will model how to express your feelings to your midolescent or any other important person in your life. This ability to respond by expressing how your child's behavior affects you and how you feel about it will, in time, help to resolve both the situation as well as your feelings.

Voice Journal: if writing your resentments is difficult for you, try recording your statements. Practice as many as you can record and take these to your friend or a professional counselor to critique. The point is, since this is a new skill, it's important for you to practice using it in ways you are comfortable with

Ask an objective friend or therapist to critique your statements as recommended below:

- Are you addressing the person by name?

- Is your resentment specific?

- Does your resentment contain a statement instead of a question?

- Is your resentment focused on one event?

- Are your feelings in this resentment one or more of five of these Six Basic Feelings and is it the last word of your statement? (mad-sad-afraid-ashamed-hurt)

- Is your statement clear?

- Would you be able to hear the statement and the person's feelings if you were on the receiving end?

- Would you be self-motivated to look at your behavior if you were on the receiving end of this resentment?

The more you practice reciting these statements without behaving histrionic, abusive, or withdrawn, the more effective you will be when you are using this method with your midolescent child. The point of these communication exercises is to learn how to express your feelings without causing an argument. By using this non-judgmental and non-shaming method, you will create an avenue of intimacy with your midolescent, or for that matter anyone with whom you're trying to communicate. It's important for you as a parent to remember that your intent is to communicate with your child so you can resolve situations and teach them something about their behavior. Negative criticism, blaming, or shaming in any way creates distance and doubt in their minds. By modeling a mature manner of expressing your feelings, you are showing them how to manage and express their own feelings. If done correctly and consistently, eventually your child will respond by expressing their feelings in the same healthy manner. Their next step will include modifying their behavior because there will be no reason for them to act out when their feelings are being heard and respected.

This is why I focus first on teaching parents to take ownership of how they feel. It's unproductive to blame someone else for your feelings. By taking responsibility for how you feel (mad-sad-glad-afraid-ashamed-hurt) you evoke an honest response from the listener. It also is important to be clear that the sole purpose of this first step is for a parent to learn how to express their feelings appropriately, so they can resolve how they feel. If you are sharing your feelings with your child with the purpose of getting them to change their behavior this exercise will come off as manipulation. If your child senses you are just using words in order to give a better lecture, he will discount what you're saying. Again, your motivation in communicating your feelings needs to be an exercise in taking ownership of them.

At this point you might be wondering how effective this method will be with your child. It's important to remember that your midolescent did not become the person he is overnight. It has taken years. For that reason, it will take a while for the positive expression of your emotions to sink in and for them to respond with behavior change. A rule of thumb is to give your efforts at practicing the Art of Feeling at least one week for every year of your child's life. For instance, if your midolescent is twenty-three years old, give your efforts approximately twenty-three weeks for this method to bear fruit. Should you see incremental change along the way? Of course you should, and you most likely will. But progress will be slow at first and at times success will appear only intermittently. You are seeking progress, not perfection. Progress consists of attempts to follow your model followed by lapses. Perfectionism will only produce heartache and a sense of failure in you and your child, so give it time. It is vital you see trouble as an opportunity to model how to handle your emotions, and not as failure. Progress takes time. Watch for overall growth and change, and don't be discouraged by the day-to-day reality of the difficulties of life.

Remember, behavior change in your child will follow naturally as the result of honest, open communications over time as trust is established and maintained. In the end it will be worth the effort you make.

What Comes Around, Goes Around

After you have mastered this process and are comfortable with it. Allow your child to write out and present the resentments he has with you. He must abide by the same rules and structure for his resentments as you have learned here. You may not like what he says and may not want to hear it, but be prepared to listen to his feelings. It will be a growing experience for everyone.

After he shares his resentments, do not react other than to say "thank you for sharing." Now wait at least twenty-four hours before approaching him about his resentments. This gives you time to settle in and absorb what your child was feeling. Additionally, it allows your midolescent the opportunity to experience his expression of feelings without "knee-jerk" reactions or judgments. There is no greater emotional growth experience than to tell your parent how you feel and then actually have them absorb it rather than react or judge you for it. If you don't believe me, ask yourself what it would be like if your own parent had allowed you such an opportunity. Most likely, it would have been life changing for sure.

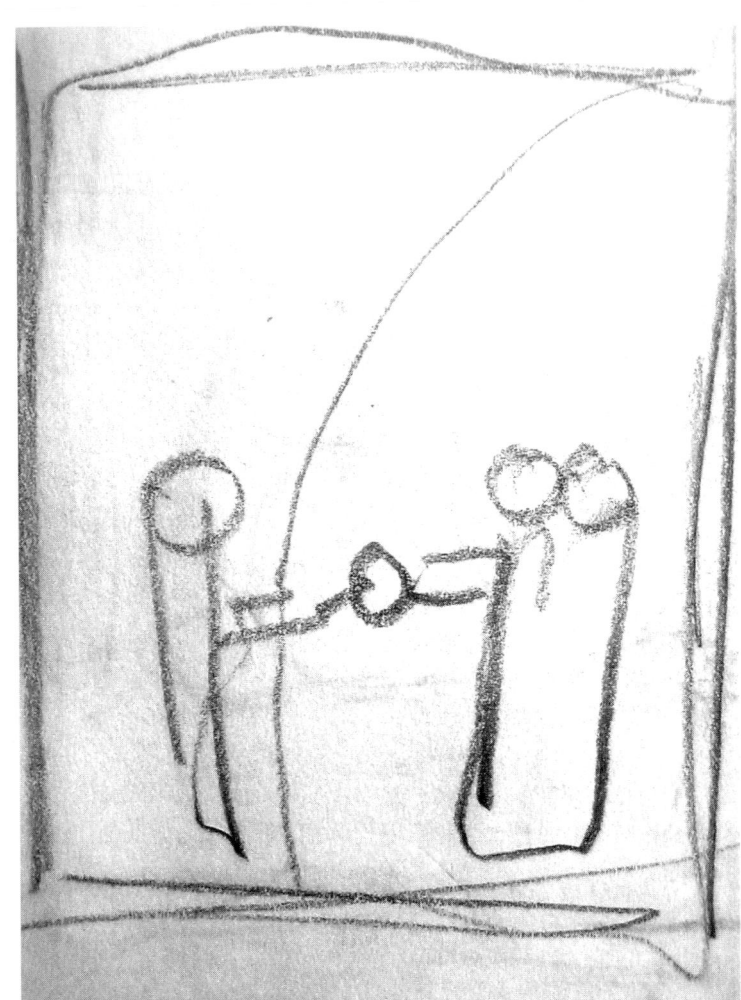

Chapter Six

Re-Directing Your Midolescent

Now that you have become familiar with the characteristics of adolescence and midolescence; the Lifespark, the Six Basic Feelings, how to deal with resentments and how to express yourself, you can move into re-directing your midolescent. First and foremost, when you do this you must do it for yourself, not for your child. Your child will quickly sniff out when you are trying to change their behavior. They will expect to hear things like "I'm doing this for your own good." That's exactly why you do it for yourself. Here's where you take a little wisdom from Alcoholics Anonymous where they say, "it's a selfish program." It's okay to take care of you for a change. Your child will respect you for it.

Think of four or five behaviors that you simply refuse to tolerate anymore from your midolescent. Write them down. It could be smoking in your home, disrespecting others by coming home at all hours of the night, not getting a job or attending college, drinking or taking drugs, etc. Remember these are behaviors that you refuse any longer to tolerate.

You may find yourself listing ten, fifteen, or twenty behaviors that bother you. You and your spouse/

partner must decide together which five you can't live with anymore. These five concerns will be written into a behavioral contract. It is imperative that included in the first thirty-days of your contract your list is whittled down to a maximum of five unacceptable behaviors. If you included every one of your concerns in your first contract, it would be overwhelming for both you and your midolescent to follow. Listing multiple concerns would set your midolescent up for failure. The primary function of the contract is to create an environment of success so he can learn tools for resolving problems. It is unreasonable to think that before your child leaves your home you will resolve every one of his behavior issues. But your goal is to equip him with tools to solve his problems for himself. This is setting your child up to succeed.

That is the reason you start your first contract with a maximum of five issues with escalating consequences. That doesn't mean you stop asking your child to clean her room if that one isn't on the list, it just means having a dirty room is not a make or break behavior.

Once you and your spouse have agreed on the four or five behaviors you will no longer tolerate, you will write a detailed plan on how your midolescent will be able to accomplish this. All too often parents react and assign tasks or give ultimatums to their child when she does not posses the tools to accomplish them. For instance, have you ever assigned your child to take out the trash and failed to mention the time period in which he has to complete the chore? What typically happens is there is an argument about when it was supposed to have been done or it doesn't get done at all. Therefore, it is your task as a parent to re-direct your midolescent every step of the way in order to accomplish your goals. You have to be willing to go to any emotional age with your child. If your child is twenty-eight going on thirteen, what would you do for a thirteen-year-old?

If he can complete these tasks as you laid them out for him, he will begin to experience a sense of accomplishment. If he can maintain this momentum, it will be no time at all before your child will begin to grow into his own life.

Before You Start

One non-negotiable item every contract should include is that there will be no drinking alcohol during the first thirty days. If your child fights you on this one, then you must assume he has a problem with alcohol. Your bottom line should be that if he is caught drinking during the thirty day period he will go into a treatment program. If he insists he can quit drinking at any time and that his drinking really isn't a problem, then there should be no problem with him quitting for thirty days. If he uses any other substances such as pot, methamphetamine, cocaine, or abuses prescription medication during this period, you can assume he is either replacing the alcohol with other mood-altering chemicals or he has a dual addiction. In either case, you must insist on treatment. Attempting to be rational with a person who is addicted to drugs or alcohol is irrational on your part. And anything you attempt to accomplish with his behavior while he is in active addiction will end in failure.

If you know your child has an ongoing drug and/or alcohol problem, this has to be solved first so the child can be emotionally present while you are trying to work with them. Self-medicating allows them to escape from taking responsibility for their behavior and their feelings. It allows them to hide from you emotionally. If you merely suspect they have a problem, this contract will be a good opportunity to get it out in the open. I suggest you add random, unannounced drug testing to the contract whenever drug or alcohol abuse is suspected.

Road Map to Success

Below, I have created a roadmap for you to follow when developing a growth plan for your midolescent. Each of your concerns should include:

1. What specific behavior you have determined you will no longer tolerate.

2. The short term goal.

3. The long term goal.

4. Steps you will take and timeline in reaching the short term goal on each item.

5. Your "bottom line" on each item.

Example:

Behavior problem: Refuses to get a job.

Short term goal: Become employed full time.

Long term goal: Become financially self-sufficient.

Specific steps to reach short-term goal:

1. Beginning tomorrow morning and everyday thereafter, you will leave the house by 8:00 am and apply for a job with at least five different companies.

2. You may not return before 3:00 pm or before you visit five companies. You must have five job applications in hand or if you applied while there, record the company name, telephone number, address, the manager's name who interviewed you, and the results of the interview. Also, a specific day you are to follow-up with the manager.

3. We will assist you in filling out the applications if need be and we will assist you online if you are applying that way. (If your child is unsure how to proceed, you can agree to drive him around for the first few days to a list of businesses where he can apply. At this point in

your child's life, if employment has been a continuing problem, remember he's not looking for a career but simply a job: fast food, construction labor, grocery bagger, or video store clerks are typical starter jobs.)

Bottom line: We will no longer tolerate you not working. You have two work-weeks to become employed full-time or you must leave the house and live somewhere else.

This plan has some meat to it, yet it is supportive. You must be willing to follow-through with your bottom line if your midolescent fails to follow-through with his end of the bargain. You don't have to throw him out the first day if he only brings home four applications; however, you must have a serious talk and let him know two more days like that and you will have to implement your bottom line.

In reality, the most difficult part for parents of midolescents is implementing their bottom line. This is where it would be a good time for you to find a support system for yourself. If you are a parent who couldn't imagine seeing your child without a roof over her head, and she knows you'll never implement a bottom line of her having to leave your home, be careful not to set yourself up for failure. Have an alternative arrangement for her that has been agreed upon in advance. This way you can implement the consequence with the least emotional trauma to yourself.

Research transitional homes, sober living homes, drug or alcohol treatment centers (if this is appropriate for your child) or even a relative who you trust will not enable your child's problem behavior, as a place for her to go if she doesn't live up to her end of the agreement in your home. The worst thing you can do to your credibility as a parent, and to your own self-respect, is to have her agree to a consequence you could never impose. There is no reason to set yourself-up to fail. Create a support structure around you by doing some basic research. For instance in the community where I live, Orange County, California, we have a network of shelters, from the traditional homeless shelter such as a rescue mission to transitional homes that have sixty-to-ninety-day programs that allow individuals going through personal difficulties to get back on their feet.

Homeless shelters such as rescue missions, which you can find in most urban areas, usually attract the hardcore homeless. Transitional shelters have similar programs, but some are even more structured than the contract we are now discussing. They are regimented and have requirements for continuing to stay in the home. Their services are designed to make their clients independent, fully functioning adults, provided they work the program. Look in your phone book, call a church or county mental health services in your community for some referrals. If a trusted relative you know will not indulge or enable your child is an option, this could be an even better scenario.

I can't emphasize enough that if you know your child has a drinking or drug problem, your contract must include a no drinking or drug use clause at least during the first thirty days of the contract. Getting them to agree to a treatment program if they break their contract is a must in your bottom-line plan.

Next Example:

Behavior problem: Refuses to be home at a decent hour.

Short term goal: Be home at an acceptable time for all family members.

Long term goal: Become respectful of others and set boundaries in your life.

Specific steps to reach short term goal:

Beginning tonight and every weeknight hereafter, you agree to be in the house no later than 10:00 P.M. On Friday and Saturday nights you agree to be in the house by 12:30 A.M., unless other arrangements have been agreed upon by all of us in advance.

Bottom line: We will no longer tolerate you coming in at all hours. We have no interest in controlling you, however, we expect you to respect that we have to get up in the morning and that we refuse to stay up worrying about you. The door will be locked at 10:10 P.M. when we go to bed. If you are not in the house you will sleep elsewhere. If it happens more than three times in one month, you must move out.

This is a reasonable expectation for any midolescent, or any family member for that matter. Do you stay out until 2:00 A.M. every morning and then go to work each day? Not likely. Then why should anybody else get away with it in YOUR house? Your hope is that if he is in by 10:00 P.M., he will be out by 7:00 A.M. to work and onto adulthood.

Next Example:

Behavior problem: Drinking in our home.

Short term goal: Stop drinking in our home.

Long term goal: Respect and appreciate others' space. Also, evaluate your drinking.

Specific steps to reach short term goal: Beginning immediately you agree to stop drinking in our home. If you drink again in our home you will stop drinking altogether and attend counseling of our choice. If you continue to drink despite this intervention, you will enter a residential treatment center and complete the program per its recommendations and our wishes. Additionally, you will not come home with alcohol on your breath.

Bottom line: We will no longer tolerate you drinking in our home or coming home smelling of alcohol. If you fail to abide by the above plan as it is laid out, you must move out immediately and we will not assist you financially.

Re-directing your midolescent will take some work on your part. It is never easy to convince your child to change his behavior and grow up. However, the alternative is to let him live with you and continue to spin out-of-control. Following the format I have outlined will give you the formal warning system and the guide necessary to help you re-direct your midolescent in as guilt-free a manner as possible. If you do everything you can to help your midolescent change and grow, you can't do any more than that. He must take the responsibility to move on, and you as a parent must be willing to place the responsibility for his growth squarely on his shoulders. Whether or not he succeeds in your plan, he will grow, as will his respect for you. One question I urge parents to ask themselves in order to avoid the inevitable guilty conscience that arises for asking a child to leave their home is: "Have I done everything I could have possibly done to support my child before asking him to leave?"

If you answered "yes" to that, then you need to place most responsibility for your child's behavior on their shoulders.

Mechanics of the Contract

Contracts must always be in writing. Contracts are short-term solutions. Your midolescent will not follow a contract for more than a few months at best. That's okay. It gives you both a jump start on new behavior. Narrow it down to five behaviors as we discussed above, the five you simply cannot live with any longer. You are not going to fight with him over his dirty room, but he's not going to smoke pot anymore. Keep in mind that this contract is the stepping stone to your success as a parent in launching your child. It is not designed to solve every problem with do or die consequences. Part of the strategy of choosing only five behaviors is not to confuse things. You are teaching them how to use emotional tools to solve their own problems. You have to be realistic that when your child launches out on their own, they are not going to be problem free. But you will have a greater peace of mind if you know they are equipped to deal with their own problems and won't be calling you every hour to solve their problems for them.

A well-written contract gives room for the growth process. That's why you don't want to write, "Clean your room or you have to leave the house." This makes no provision for imperfection. And again, going back to our chapter on the Lifespark, this sense that a child has to be perfect, has to live up to every one of your expectations perfectly, damages their Lifespark and creates a sense that unless they're perfect they won't be accepted. A child enslaved to a sense of perfection is just as damaged as the child mired in their own sense of failure.

Be Prepared for the Crisis

You must prepare yourself for the inevitable. Sometime during the first thirty days, your child will break one of the rules and earn a consequence. Let's say that one of the issues in your child's contract is drinking, and your midolescent comes home with alcohol on his breath. Are you going to throw him out? It depends on your contract. If he's over twenty-one (which most midolescents are), and wasn't driving and just had a beer with his friend, maybe not. But let's say this is the third time, and your contract had a "no-drinking period" clause. Your child will feel desperate and begin to argue, manipulate, and do his best to squirm out of what he knows is coming. The excuses will pile up and you will feel tempted to renegotiate the contract. Don't allow your child to talk you into changing the contract in the midst of a crisis. If he's like most midolescents, he has some well-polished excuses why he had to drink. He will plead for mercy just this one time. Some parents are especially susceptible to this because of their emotional ties to their child, which in any other case is understandable. But now the consequence you have to impose has been mutually agreed upon in advance, so follow it. If you have prepared alternative living arrangements in advance, as we discussed earlier, your child knows what's coming. Therefore the emotional turmoil and toll will be reduced. Sticking to your contract will buy you credibility and respect in the eyes of your child. It will also keep your self-respect intact.

But you also need to prepare yourself not to overreact emotionally. For instance, your child comes home drunk for the first time since signing his contract. Your contract calls for a three-strike rule. But you're angry and you've had enough, so you tell him, "I don't care what the contract says; I want you out of the house right now." You've now broken the contract and are treating your child unfairly. You have to be as reliable and consistent as you expect your child to be. Again by honoring the contract, you will gain respect and credibility in their eyes. This contract will protect you from your child's manipulation and will help put a boundary on one's natural tendencies to react. You have to leave room for failure and imperfection so they can learn and grow from their mistakes.

You can always sit down and negotiate the overall plan but never the contract, particularly in the midst of a crisis.

If you know that you are subject to manipulation by your midolescent and need some additional support, get an objective third party to sign onto the contract with you and your child. This could be a relative or family friend that you can trust who isn't easily manipulated. That third person, a sister, brother, brother-in-law, uncle, etc., can act as final arbiter, when it comes down to enforcing a consequence. You have to guard yourself from those moments of crisis where the emotion of a situation will blur your better judgment. By including a third party who is removed from the emotional heat of the situation, you can take the pressure off yourself. This would be a good plan for single parents, both mothers and fathers, who feel they easily get twisted up in the emotional clutter of disciplinary situations.

The third party will witness and sign the agreement and then in the middle of an intense situation you can call them and explain the situation. Both sides could tell their stories and the third party can rule. This creates an emotional safety valve for the parent and will leave you less susceptible to manipulation.

The Second Thirty Days

The initial thirty-day contract is initiated by the parents, with no input from your child in order to resolve the five most burdensome problems. If the child holds to the contract for thirty-days then it's time to sit down with him and renegotiate another thirty-day contract. This time your midolescent is allowed to have input as to what behaviors are to change and their consequences. If your child is over twenty-one, and has proven to be responsible with alcohol the non-negotiable rule of no drinking can be reconsidered. However, you must consider that drinking has an effect on behavior, alcoholic or not. Therefore, I recommend no drinking until your midolescent leaves home. Again, if he doesn't have a drinking problem, then not drinking should not be a problem.

Consequences versus Punishment

Consequences need to be spelled out in advance in the contract. The difference between consequences and punishment is something parents need to keep in mind. Consequences are agreed upon by all parties in advance. Punishment is a reaction that comes out of unresolved resentment. If you stick to the consequences you have agreed upon for any given rule, then you build trust with your child. However, if you come home from a rough day at the office, and toss out a harsher punishment because you're mad at all the things your child has ever done to you, you are reacting. Giving out unwarranted punishments will only lose their respect and damage your relationship. You never make threats, you make promises. Then, you keep them.

For instance, you come home after a tough day at the office and find your daughter smoking in the house, which violates your no-smoking rule in your contract. The last thing you need is to find your daughter smoking in your home, especially when she knows smoking is off limits for everyone. You snap and take the cigarettes and throw them down the toilet and tell her to get out of the house right now and find somewhere else to live. If the consequences spelled out in your contract said she could no longer smoke anywhere on the property if caught smoking in the house, you now are measuring out punishment and not consequences. Again, by following through with the contract and the agreed upon consequences you will build trust and gain credibility with your child. And this is one of the most important benefits of working with your midolescent through the use of a contract—to build trust and credibility as a parent in the eyes of your child.

What if I Can't Let Go?

What if you've done everything we have talked about and now it's time for your child to leave the house and start his own life, but you can't let go. You know the contract calls for them to leave your home, but you can't do it. You need to ask yourself the question, what is it about my own history that won't allow me to let go of my child? At this point your issues are probably not with your child and her behaviors, but with your own history. What is it about you that would make you think your child will not survive if you are not there to cook breakfast for her or to do her laundry?

My best advice is to go into therapy with an agenda to discover why you can't let go. A good therapist should help you get some resolution in six to ten sessions. By taking a look at your own adolescence you'll probably find that some element of your Lifespark was damaged. What if you were abandoned by your parents and you resolved to never do this to your child? And now you've created a worse situation and you are destroying your child. The more desperate you feel as a parent the more you need to examine what you are doing to add to this sense of desperation. A productive therapy experience will allow you to grow and give you insight into your relationship with your child and also with yourself.

Expect Emotional Growth

Continue to use the Six Basic Feelings. Keep a list of the feelings: mad-sad-glad-afraid-ashamed-hurt in front of you at all times. When your child is having difficulty with any of your rules, get them to express how they're feeling. For instance, your midolescent needs to get a job.

He says: "I don't think I can find a job."

You say: "It sounds like you're afraid." By reflecting back and guessing how he feels, you get him out of his head and into his heart. This way you can zero-in on the real issue, which is his fear. What if he is rejected for a job by everyone? Here is your chance to give your son some emotional support. It's important to get down to what a person is feeling. You need to acknowledge his feelings but stick with the contract. The Six Basic Feelings remind you that the important underlying issue is not what your child thinks, but how he feels. Be sure to validate his feelings, regardless of whether or not you agree with his way of thinking or his behavior. Again, acknowledge his feelings and stick with the contract.

You say: "I know you're afraid, but I no longer will allow you to live here without a job. You have ___ days to become employed. If you want to discuss your fears, I am here for you and I will listen."

The Consequences of Not Following Through

The long term goal of the contract is to get your child to live independently. Independence won't happen overnight so you must be prepared that it may take a year or more for them to gain the skills and confidence they need to strike out on their own. During this year you will be tested, stressed out, frustrated, sad, and often angry. You might wish he would just go back to doing what he was doing before, lying on the sofa, just getting by. But you must keep in mind that there are consequences to you, your spouse, and your family for not following through—just as there are positive consequences of following through, such as watching your child grow and become a functioning, self-supporting, emotionally healthy adult. Consequences both positive and negative impact not just your child, but you and the rest of your family as well.

It is important to consider what will happen to you as a person if you don't follow through. The situation with your child will continue to cause fights between you and your spouse, between you and your other children. It will destroy your own sense of serenity. You already fear that your child will not survive in the world. The prolonged tension in the family could send you over the edge into your own addictive behavior. It could destroy your marriage, your health, your spirituality, and you relationships at work.

But when you follow through with your contract, you will strengthen yourself emotionally, spiritually, and physically. The benefits of following through will be life-changing and life-affirming for you and all of your relationships.

Chapter Seven

Creating the Controlled Conflict

It was Sir Isaac Newton who first articulated the laws of motion, which said that a "body at rest tends to stay at rest." Newton didn't have midolescents in mind when he first developed his laws of motion, but in some ways it easily illustrates the emotional state of your child. Parents of midolescents know the truth of this statement. A midolescent by nature has found a comfortable equilibrium in your home. His out of whack life has found a dysfunctional way to balance itself, all at your expense. He's found a place where he's taken care of, and his life is manageable on his terms. He can block out the real world of responsibility, of growth, of disappointment and difficulties through whatever medication of choice you're allowing him to use in your home. It may be TV, it may be drugs, legal or illegal, and it may be alcohol or sex or video games. Whatever he's doing, he's found a way to quell his inner turmoil so he doesn't have to face his feelings. And in its place he's created a manageable existence, one that does not include working, taking responsibility for himself, or for those around him. All of these accountabilities would require him to experience some stress, conflict, and challenge. And your midolescent has found a way around all of these situations. He's a body at rest—emotionally.

And except for the stress it causes you when you think about how you're being taken advantage of, or when you dwell on your fears that he is going to kill himself in some way, both of your lives work and will continue to do so—if you let them. The purpose of this book is to teach parents how to express their feelings and learning this skill will help your child understand and express theirs. I have led you to believe this communication skill will solve your child's lack of motivation and teach him responsibility, which is true. But what I haven't told you is that as soon as you sign the contract we discussed in the previous chapter, your life and your midolescent's life are going to change—radically. You have consciously created a controlled inner conflict within your child, and you need to expect all the fallout that will ensue. You have knocked his world off kilter, destroyed the safe haven he's hidden in and forced him to face how he truly feels inside. You need to be prepared for the difficulties that change will cause in your home. The good news here is that your child has you, a caring parent or caregiver, to guide him through this inner conflict.

This "controlled conflict" can be the most chilling aspect for most parents. No loving parent wants to knowingly harm their child and at times, once the contract is in place, your child may howl like a wounded cub and bring every ounce of your maternal and paternal instincts to the surface of your life. Parents during this time of conflict need to remind themselves of who they are and what they are doing. Therefore, I have developed the following list that will help parents reassure themselves they are doing the right thing. Ask yourself the following questions:

- Am I providing food?

- Am I providing shelter?

- Is he/she safe in my home?

- Am I providing supervision and love?

- Am I providing professional counseling or medical care if necessary?

- Am I doing this all out of genuine concern and not toxic anger, fear, or shame?

If you can say "yes" to the above, I assure you, you can shake the tree all you want and you and your child will be okay. Your child is not on the streets; he's not hungry or going around in rags and your home is safe and has clear boundaries. You are a good parent. If you are withholding any of the above, like water and food, genuine concern, or have an unsafe home, you need to correct those things immediately.

I suggest you put these questions on your dresser mirror and keep asking them of yourself during the tough times. It's okay to reassure yourself you are doing the right thing.

By enforcing the contract your child will begin to feel things he's blocked or denied for a long time, probably his whole life. Expect that he will fumble, have difficulties, express himself inappropriately, and go through a readjusting period to the new reality in your home. You have taken a body at rest and shoved him in the direction of change and growth. He has lost the easy balance he had in his life and that's exactly what you wanted to happen. His feelings will be stirred. Expect that he will not like it. What couch potato likes having the remote taken out of his hand and being told to get a job? Or being told he can't drink or smoke pot in your home? He's now a body in motion armed with a set of feelings he has successfully suppressed with your complicity. In every sense, he is armed and dangerous. While by "dangerous" I mean emotionally volatile, not physically threatening, if at any time you do feel physically threatened by your child, don't hesitate to call the police. If you have to do that one time, more than likely it will not happen again. You've set your bottom line and boundary and he knows it must not be crossed.

Your midolescent is going to become uncomfortable when you write and assign the contract. But the real test comes when you have to enforce it. The contract is the catalyst to moving your child along emotionally. The good news is when your midolescent is challenged with your new expectations and you follow through with the agreed upon consequences, he will begin to resist. What's good about that, you may ask? Oppositional behavior is expected, and therefore you can view it as progress. You just have to change your idea of what "progress" looks like. In therapy, the counselor always looks for the resistance when new behaviors are tried out by the client. It is normal. The therapist doesn't think he's a failure just because the client didn't follow-through with the new behavior or failed at certain aspects of the assignment. After all, fallibility is one of the characteristics of our Lifespark. So, as a parent, allow your child the dignity to fail and experience his feelings. Don't rescue him at the moment he needs you most to allow him to grow. That moment of growth comes most significantly when he is struggling to feel. So here are a few healthy signs of growing pains you should expect when your midolescent is faced with change:

OPPOSITION—We all become oppositional and resistant when we have to come out of our routine or comfort zone. This is natural. Let your child experience the feelings that accompany change. Don't engage in an argument or a pity party; this is a form of rescue and your child will not learn or grow without legitimate suffering.

AGGRESSION—This is born out of frustration from being awkward trying on a new behavior (such as taking "no" for an answer from dad). It is natural that a person would become angry about change. Don't allow aggressive behavior to deter your intentions. Simply acknowledge your child's frustration, take a deep breath and leave the room. Your child and you will live through it.

MANIPULATION—This comes in all forms and you as the parent are all too familiar with your child's different styles of manipulation. Point it out to your child when you recognize it and say "when you _____ I feel _____ mad-sad-glad-afraid-ashamed-hurt." Then move on to something productive. Never engage in a conversation when your child attempts an obvious manipulation. Example: "I sense you are attempting to manipulate me right now and that's disrespectful to both of us. I feel sad." Then leave the room. Leave your child with the feelings.

BARGAINING—When all else fails expect your child will attempt to bargain with you to change the contract. Again, call it as you see it and say, "I won't bargain with you about your life. It's too valuable. I feel hurt." Then leave the room and leave your child to experience his feelings without interruption.

DENIAL—Denial is sincere delusion. Your child is full of denial from living outside of his value system. He probably believes his own lies even if they appear unbelievable to everyone else. When you recognize this defense mechanism, point it out. Tell your child that you don't see things that way, and that he needs to look at things (at least for the next thirty-days) from your perspective. Tell him, "It appears that you are in denial or don't see what I see. I feel sad and afraid." Leave the room.

ACCEPTANCE—Ah! When your midolescent gets to this point on any given issue of his contract you can be sure that he will fall back into denial. However, continue to enforce the contact and don't negotiate with your child. He will eventually or even suddenly reach the goal of acceptance, at which time you can say, "I feel glad."

Above all, remember that these are normal reactions as a result of consistently enforcing the contract and expressing your feelings at every chance you get. Keep looking for "progress not perfection."

Be assured that in my thirty-plus years working with teenagers and young adults, I have never seen a work in progress that didn't include these elements. If your child doesn't react at all, he's not changing. Stay on track when you see these indicators. It's definitely working.

When your midolescent fails to adhere to the contract

It's inevitable that problems will arise. By now you know to expect them because your child has had his feelings stirred up. Your main task now in dealing with him regarding his contract is to assist him in separating his thoughts from his feelings. (Review again the section in chapter four on separating feelings, thoughts, and behaviors for a more detailed explanation of this process.) I have outlined some scenarios below and detailed how this works in each one. Again, keep in mind that progress is our goal, not perfection. When problems arise with the contract, be flexible but committed. It is likely you have no credibility with your child at this point because he has manipulated you and you have probably enabled him for quite some time. You will need to earn his respect. As I discussed earlier never negotiate a behavioral contract in a crisis. But recognize you wrote the contract to deal with that specific behavior with which you're now having difficulties. You now have come to your child's primary growth opportunity. Help him through it and you will help him move on.

Example Problem: The contract states "no smoking in my house" and you just caught your son smoking in his room.

Mom: "Randy, you broke your agreement not to smoke in my house. I feel hurt, mad, and sad. It's time to sit down and implement the consequence we all agreed upon. I have faith you will grow from this experience and I expect that it will not happen again."

Mom implements the consequence.

Randy: "This isn't fair. I wasn't thinking. Can't we just bypass this one?"

Mom: "Randy, you sound mad and afraid. I would appreciate you expressing your feelings directly with me instead of telling me what you're thinking. Remember, we all agreed to the contract to help you reach your goal of moving out of the house. I am keeping my promise to you."

Mom leaves the room. Randy has his consequence and his feelings. Both are positive.

Example Problem: It has been two weeks and Randy has not gotten a job as agreed.

Mom: "Randy, you, I, and your father are meeting at 6 p.m. tonight to enforce the consequence for not getting a job. You do not seem to be taking this seriously. I feel mad, sad, ashamed, and hurt."

Randy: "I am serious. I just can't get a job."

Mom: "You sound mad or ashamed about that."

Randy: "I do feel ashamed."

Mom: "I appreciate you sharing your feelings. However, we must implement the consequence and we will work toward a solution tonight."

Had Randy not verbalized his feelings, Mom could have engaged him with the "Hamster Wheel" technique until he did. At this point, getting Randy to share his feelings is more important than strategizing on how to get a job.

Hamster Wheel Technique

This technique should be used when you sense a threat, argument, negotiation, or any other form of manipulation coming on. Your child, at times, will attempt to wear you down by continually asking, pleading, negotiating with you to break the contract, or asking for a special favor. They might want to attend a concert, hang out with friends that are off limits, delay getting a job, or whatever the issue may be. So they keep hounding you with the same request because this has worked for them in the past. To use the Hamster Wheel technique you simply keep going around and around with three impressions: His feeling(s), your feeling(s), and the contract—until the end result is about feelings. For instance:

1. **HIS FEELINGS:** If you are not sure about how your child is feeling, guess at it based on his behavior or what he says. Now "reflect" or verbalize what you think your child is feeling: "You sound mad or ashamed." Don't make absolute statements such as "you are mad." Nobody really knows what another person is feeling until they verbalize it.

2. **YOUR FEELINGS:** Express your own feelings: "You seem lost to me; I feel sad."

3. **THE CONTRACT:** Enforce it: "We're going to stick to what we agreed upon in the contract."

4. Leave the room ASAP after enforcing the contract.

Example Problem: Randy breaks the contract.

Randy: "Mom, can't we just let it go this time?"

Mom: "It sounds like you feel sad and ashamed."

Randy: "Exactly. Now can't we let this one go?"

Mom: "Randy you broke your agreement. I feel sad. Thank goodness we have the contract to guide us through this." Mom leaves the room.

Notice in this scenario Mom keeps her responses short, simple, and on point: feelings, feelings, contract. Then she leaves the room. Mom does not stand around waiting for the rebound comment from her child. Rather, she leaves her child alone to reflect on his behavior and how he feels. In your own situation it's helpful to have a list of the Six Basic Feelings in sight at all times for you and your child to see and to use.

Reflecting your feelings is not always necessary. For example, the third time your child asks to go to the concert, after you've already said no twice, you don't need to keep reflecting his feelings. You've already done that and you both know he's mad. Here it's acceptable for you to express your feelings. "I've already told you it's not okay for you to go to the concert. Now you're not respecting my boundaries. I feel mad." Walk away.

This re-establishes your boundaries and forces your child to start being respectful. When you stick to your truth and refuse to be manipulated your child will eventually come out of their denial and begin to grow.   If these exercises don't work, you need to get help from a professional counselor. Stick to the book and the plan, but use the counselor to reinforce your goals and the plan.

How do you know your child is "getting it?"

You know they're "getting it" when you begin to hear their feelings. Your child will express mostly anger because that's the easiest and most acceptable feeling to express. Your job is to interpret their words and/or behavior and reflect back their feelings. Even if they behave as though its anger, it usually isn't. Guess at the feeling, reflect it back. What's most important, however, is that as long as your child is expressing feelings, he's making progress. Don't listen to what's said, such as, "I'm going to leave" or "I hate you." Rather listen for the underlying feelings.

Is your child practicing the format of expressing his feelings? If not, remind them to do so. You can encourage them to read this book or the chapter on resentments to understand the process you're following. Your child is typically not going to say she's ashamed or hurt, but it would be significant progress if she did.

Continue to reflect their feelings and don't get hung up on their words. Their words will do nothing but engage you in an argument. So when your child says to you, "That's a stupid idea. I'm not going to that picnic." You could reflect back, "It sounds like you're afraid." Maybe she's feeling afraid of new social situations. You know your child best, therefore, reflecting back her feelings can become second nature to you. Just don't allow her to engage you with meaningless words. If words are getting heated, don't allow them to affect you. State how her behavior affects your feelings, then leave the room.

But always remember to listen for the child's underlying feeling. If you think your daughter is sounding afraid, tell her. Let her come back and tell you how she was feeling if you were wrong. By helping your child examine what she's feeling you're helping her understand her motivations and her behavior. So be assured that behind all the inflammatory words are feelings. It would even be a good idea to let your child know you're going to work to guess at her feelings if she's not expressing them to you. This may help to motivate her to express herself.

Look for the little changes that indicate steps of progress. Your child will begin to:

- have fewer problems with the contract
- be more joyful
- listen better
- argue less
- be less impulsive
- express her feelings respectfully
- respond rather than react
- let go of resentments
- engage you in small talk
- be less defensive
- take initiative even in the little things
- use the Six Basic Feelings words

- talk to both parents and avoid splitting them
- meet their personal emotional needs
- attend self-help type meetings
- develop more healthy relationships outside the family
- spend less time at home

Your child's life up to this point has been designed around avoiding his feelings. Deep down your child needs to express them. However, at this point his life is shallow and he is focused on material things as a way of avoiding his feelings. He probably wants what he wants and is willing to manipulate you to get it. And you have probably given it to him. What does your child really have to lose here? Why can't he go find a girl to live with who has her own place and a nice car and manipulate her? Because a girl who has her own apartment and a new car is not important enough. What your child needs is to be acknowledged and validated by his primary caregivers. And that's you. He may find a girl or friends to manipulate. But usually he will find his way back home again because they can't meet his needs. You can meet his needs by using the Six Basic Feelings in the way I have described.

Expect emotional growth. If you expect less, you'll get less. If you expect more, you'll get more. Be open and honest with your child about your plans. Hand this book to them and ask them to read it. Secrets are what keep us stuck and keep us sick. Manipulation only works when we have secrets. The more you are transparent about your motives and your plans, the less you are able to be manipulated. Once you are no longer susceptible to being manipulated the rules in your home will change. Your transparency will also be an example to your child of the power of open communication.

Above all, be true to yourself. Stay true to what I have laid out here. Resist the urge to indulge in long lectures. Lectures can never resolve their feelings. Only your child can resolve his own feelings. He will learn to resolve them for himself as you show him how. Don't stray from what has worked for so many others: Always acknowledge your child's feelings; express your feelings to them; and reaffirm your commitment to the contract; and always use the Six Basic Feelings and you will see remarkable growth, not only in your child, but also in every one of your relationships.

Chapter 8

Intervention—When All Else Fails

If you have practiced the principles in this book for several weeks and yet find no response from your adolescent or midolescent, it could be due to extensive drug or alcohol abuse or complicated psychiatric conditions. In either case, drastic behavior requires a rapid response. There is still hope, but you must act now. It's called intervention.

Midolescents with these complicated and life threatening problems must be convinced at once to seek professional help. Intervention is the process that's used to convince them they need help. The original process of intervention was created by Vernon Johnson. Mr. Johnson encountered great frustration while attempting to convince alcoholics to seek treatment. He eventually designed a sure-fire way to insure that when a person needs professional help, he was able to get them into a treatment center with a phenomenal success rate of ninety-six percent. Even today, interventions work at a ninety percent success rate.

Intervention in this case consists of a trained professional guiding the midolescents family and friends through a process that results in an immediate admission into a treatment center. The interventionist sits down with the family and friends in a confidential setting without the knowledge of the midolescent who is about to be confronted. The interventionist educates them about addiction, co-existing psychological disorders and the roles they each should assume during the intervention. All parties involved are taught to present specific, self-destructive behavior that they have observed of the midolescent over a particular period of time. The information is presented in a direct, yet loving manner that confronts the midolescent in a way that overwhelms his denial system. The parties involved might even role-play the intervention prior to the real thing. Again, the goal is to set up a situation that will convince the loved one to enter treatment.

Midolescents are experts at hiding the truth from their parents for a variety of reasons. And it's easy for them to convince their parents that everything is okay. As parents, it is natural to want to believe and protect our children, regardless of their age. Therefore, we tend to ease back into denial and "back off" in a situation when we should take immediate action. That "gut reaction" that something is deeply wrong with our child never leaves us as parents. We live the emotional nightmare and walk the emotional mine field around our child from the day we sense trouble. We are always wondering and worrying.

I have personally met all too many parents who have lost their child emotionally, psychologically, or even to death who told me, "If only we had gone with our gut and acted right away."

I am a thirty-year veteran-adolescent specialist who trained at the Johnson Institute. As an interventionist, I experienced a different frustration than that of Mr. Johnson while working with parents of troubled teenagers. My frustration led me to develop specialized techniques that are extremely effective with the adolescent and midolescent population.

If you have reached a breaking point and you need immediate assistance, you can contact me by logging onto my website www.teensavers.com and fill out the information forms, or you can choose to reach me direct: Toll Free 1-800-451-1947. Either way, you will change your midolescents life if you use the process described in this book or decide to use the services of an interventionist.

Epilogue

Perhaps you're interested in why I wrote this book or what inspired me. The answer is I was a midolescent myself. My life was out-of-control, purposeless and I had no *self* during my adolescence. I merely existed all the way up to age twenty-five, and to this day I can pinpoint the day I became an adult. I had been a "perfect" teenager up to age fifteen when my brother, Gary, was killed in Vietnam. Gary had always been the high achiever in the family, the golden boy. The day we received the news of his death my family was devastated. We never talked about his death, even during the funeral. I felt deep shame. This was a governing scene in my life.

I began to drink alcohol and after the very first drink I loved what it did for me. It was all downhill from there. I barely passed high school. As a matter-of-fact, I couldn't tell you one thing significant about my high school or any kid who attended. I was not present there or anywhere else in my life during that time. After graduation, I joined the Air Force and left for basic training within two weeks. I later became a police officer, yet during my stint in the service I spent more time in the brig than anyone I ever arrested. This was all due to my drinking, which was by now full blown alcoholism.

They "excused" me from service and I went back home accompanied by my worst enemy—me. I continued along this same path in and out of jails and rehabs (seven to be exact). Every treatment program I entered taught me about the "disease" of alcoholism and that A.A. was the only thing that could save my life. The problem was, nobody realized (including me) that I was a midolescent, that I had no clearly defined *self* and that if I didn't get in touch with and deal with my feelings, as well as control my behavior nothing was going to change.

The good news is that my parents refused to enable me by giving me a warm bed and food or money. It was tougher on my parents because I could live under stairwells and eat potato chips for breakfast (when I could find the dime), and I thought that was fine. I was so far out-of-touch with myself that alcohol, drugs, and unemployment were normal to me and I found plenty of low-level friends who validated my belief. My parents suffered, watching their son deteriorate. But they did the right thing. They told me they would help me as soon as I entered treatment again and stayed clean and sober long enough for them to trust me.

I entered into a treatment center for the last time on May 6, 1978. I have been clean and sober ever since. But the greatest thing that happened to me in this last program was that I was forced to look at my behavior (as you can do for your midolescent in your contract in this book) and they taught me the language of feelings (which I have taught you in this book). Your child may also need some time in rehab. If that's the case, its money well spent. Any other money you give to your child is enabling him to continue his self-destructive behavior.

The tools for recovery from any emotional issue are at your disposal in this book. You simply need the courage to follow the guide here and to love your child enough to not like or condone his behavior. You must also deal with your own feelings. If you practice the principles in this book on a daily basis, your feelings should come naturally in about a month.

I wish your family well and I know this will work for you if you stay with it. Remember—"progress, not perfection."

Timothy Chapman, Msc.D., C.S.A.C.

Appendix One
Assessment Guide

Assessing: ADHD
(Attention Deficit Hyperactivity Disorder)

When comparing my child to kids of the same age, he/she:

_____ constantly fidgets with his/her hands and feet

_____ often squirms and has difficulty remaining seated

_____ is easily distracted

_____ has difficulty following through on most things

_____ talks excessively

_____ often interrupts or intrudes on others

_____ doesn't listen

_____ is constantly losing things

_____ seems unaware of others around him/her

_____ has little or no patience

Many parents and children have lived with the nightmare of ADHD, suffering years of frustration. It may be the reason your child is acting-out in school or seems to have a learning disability. However, ADHD symptoms may also mimic or cover up other conditions. If you checked four or more I recommend you get a professional assessment.

ADHD Home Remedy

Gain as much information as possible on this subject. Keep in mind, your child could be suffering ADHD and other issues as well. For instance, it is common for an ADHD child to also be abusing substances and both conditions must be addressed. However, the substance abuse must be addressed immediately.

If your child is ADHD:

- Set measurable short term tasks and goals for him.
- Praise productive behavior.
- Play down or ignore the negative behavior as much as possible.
- Keep a chart or reminder list in sight for your child.
- Include a check off list with the chart.
- Develop a behavior contract. Include benefits and consequences for positive and negative behavior.
- Enroll your child in counseling. Group therapy is probably the most productive for ADHD children.
- Enter therapy yourself. You are on an emotional roller coaster.

- Learn to laugh at your frustrations. Humor is important.

- Use the Six Basic Feelings (mad-sad-glad-afraid-ashamed-hurt) when communicating with your teen. It will simplify everything.

Assessing: Anger & Resentment

Resentments are unresolved feelings and are not always about anger. It could be any one of the Six Basic Feelings that have not been resolved. Resentments can be unresolved feelings from twenty years or two days ago.

My child:

_____ rarely expresses his/her anger in a direct way

_____ takes his/her anger out on younger siblings

_____ is upset with me and won't admit it

_____ lies when it's just as easy to tell the truth

_____ exhibits covert signs of anger (says "yes," means "no"-smiles when feeling hurt, etc.)

_____ is often sarcastic

_____ talks behind my back

_____ steals from me

_____ procrastinatcs (puts off most tasks)

_____ deliberately does poorly in school to "get back at me"

If you checked three or more, your child has resentments that could lead to self-destructive anger problems.

Resentments Home Remedy

Get your family to practice "cleaning house" with feelings on a regular basis. This will help to eliminate resentments.

Here's how:

- Set a time for a "resentment meeting."
- There should be NO consequences for expressing resentments or feelings (appropriately) in this meeting.
- Everyone is treated equally in this meeting.
- This is a listening meeting—NO feedback.
- Everyone comes with a prepared list.

Resentments MUST be done in the following manner:

(Name, or title, i.e. mom or dad) I resent ……………..........,
I feel ……..........…….

Example: "Mom, I resent you listening in on my phone calls. I feel mad…"

Or

"Johnny, I resent that you were given your allowance in advance this week and then you didn't finish your chores. I feel hurt and mad…"

Assessing: Anorexia Nervosa or Bulimia

My child:

_____ is at least 15% below his/her expected weight

_____ is underweight, yet fears getting fat

_____ is underweight, yet complains about being fat

_____ is completely obsessed about his/her body

_____ has two episodes or more of binge eating per week

_____ exercises vigorously every day

_____ self-induces vomiting

_____ is constantly on "unnecessary" diets

_____ experiences physical complications from dieting

This condition is most profound in female adolescents. It can be an extremely dangerous medical condition. It has significant psychological impact on the child and the family. If you check off more than three items on this list, I encourage a professional evaluation.

Timothy Chapman, Msc.D., C.S.A.C.

Anorexia Nervosa or Bulimia Home Remedy

If your child has an eating disorder, a loving "intervention" needs to take place.

- Collect specific data concerning your child's eating disorder.
- Write down at least seven specific instances where you are concerned about your child's well-being.
- Write how you FEEL after each instance.

Example:

"Mary, last night at dinner, you ate a large portion of food and then went into the bathroom. Everyone at the table overheard you vomiting in there. When you came out, you appeared as though nothing was wrong. I feel sad and afraid for you."

- Sit down with your child, read the prepared list and tell her you are getting her help.

- Contact a doctor or therapist who specializes in eating disorders and go along with your teen to the appointment. Bring your list of concerns.

Assessing: Inappropriate Attitude

My child:

_____ rarely shows enthusiasm anymore

144

_____ tells me one thing, and does another

_____ is the family critic (verbally or silently)

_____ resists all of my/our ideas or suggestions

_____ believes only his/her friends are right

_____ makes threats of violence

_____ lies when it's easier to tell the truth

_____ displays aggressive body language

_____ is generally rude to others

_____ rarely acknowledges or validates others

Attitude is an intimate issue. Parents are the true experts in assessing their teen's attitude. It is difficult if not unfair to "generalize" one's attitude. Every child's attitude or way of interpreting life is unique.

Inappropriate Attitude Home Remedy

When approaching your child, be careful not to "attack" his/her attitude. Adolescents have difficulty separating who they are from their attitude. Attitude is not who you are, but rather how you presently see and react to things. How you see things (especially for teenagers) is usually temporary.

- Research and uncover the underlying factors leading to your child's attitude problem. It may be unresolved feelings.

- Sit down with your child and describe your frustration about his/her attitude.

- Tell your child what you perceive and how you feel about it.

Example:

"John, I'm frustrated that you tell me it's none of my business whether or not you pass math. I feel hurt."

Using "I" statements and expressing feelings makes your point and has emotional impact. At the same time you are teaching your child the process of dealing with feelings.

Assessing: Depression

Over the past few weeks, my child:

_____ spends hours/days alone in his/her room.

_____ has significant changes in eating habits

_____ exhibits a depressed or irritable mood

_____ exhibits daily insomnia or long periods of sleep

_____ experiences daily fatigue

_____ has a diminished ability to think or concentrate

_____ has all but stopped communicating

_____ made comments or suggestions about suicide

_____ lost interest in most daily activities

_____ exhibits significant weight change

Depression could be the root of other problems. Children often exhibit symptoms of depression yet deny it exists. It is the parent's role to intervene in the situation whether or not the child likes or agrees with it. You know your child's moods best.

Depression Home Remedy

Addressing depression early can save your child from a life of doom. Your child may be suffering from a "situational" depression. If you can identify the recent situation contributing to your child's depression, talk to your child using the Six Basic Feelings. If your child resists or you are not helping the situation, contact a therapist for a professional assessment. If your child has a chronic or genetic type of depression, he/she may benefit from medication. A psychiatrist is the appropriate professional to assess, prescribe, and monitor medication. As the depression dissipates the psychiatrist may decrease the dosage.

Never rely on medication alone to fix the problem. Medication is merely another tool to address the depression. Sometimes medication works to stabilize a person long enough to confront and resolve a situational problem. In most cases medication is not necessary.

Your child eventually needs to address the psychological factors contributing to his/her condition.

Assessing: Feelings

I'm concerned that my child is out of touch with his/her feelings.

My child:

_____ avoids discussing feelings at all costs

_____ exhibits behavior that doesn't match the appropriate feelings (smiles when sad)

_____ turns sadness or hurt into anger

_____ denies ever feeling hurt

_____ never uses the words that describe feelings (mad-sad-glad-afraid-ashamed-hurt)

_____ engages only in intellectual conversation

_____ fears intimacy

_____ was hurt long ago, but has never dealt with it

_____ answers most "how do you feel questions" with "fine"

_____ I (mom or dad) don't know how to deal with my own feelings

Feelings are facts. What you feel is real. As mentioned throughout this book, feelings are a fact-of-life. If you don't control them, they will control you. Feelings are also a language that can heal emotional, physical, and spiritual conditions. It is necessary to connect with your child at a feeling level in order to reach intimacy.

Feelings Home Remedy

First, read and re-read this book. Practice the principles I have laid out for you. Master the techniques of dealing with feelings. Then practice "reflection" every time you speak to your child.

Example:

- Your child comes home from school and states: "I'm never going back to that school again, as long as I live."

- Your response could be: "What's the matter?" or "Yes, you are, if I have to take you there myself."

- Using reflection simplifies your response: "you sound mad."

- Next, let your child respond.

- If the response is: "Yes, I am," then go forward with the discussion.

- If the response is: "No," or "Don't tell me how to feel."

- You should respond: "OK, but you seemed mad based on your tone of voice and because you threw your book bag down on the floor. So how are you feeling?"

Assessing: Gang Activity

If recent behavior has indicated gang affiliation, check out the situation immediately.

My child has or is:

_____ dressing like a gangster

_____ pulling away from old friends and family

_____ been going out at all hours of the night with suspicious kids

_____ been detained or arrested for gang type behavior

_____ a written "code" or language of his/her own

_____ becoming dangerous

_____ stealing money or property from me or others

_____ been threatened or makes threats to others

_____ instilled a fear in me. I fear for our safety

Gang activity has reached epidemic proportion nationwide and your community is not immune. Gang members have a common ground; they serve as a family for each other.

Developing strong family values and activities is your best defense. Once a child is in a gang the prevention days are over.

Gang Activity Home Remedy

If you know your child is in a gang you need to confront the problem immediately.

Before confronting your child:

- Meet with a counselor or police officer who has experience working with gang members.
- The counselor/police officer will evaluate the level of danger and make appropriate recommendations.
- If an "intervention" is to take place, the counselor must be equipped to do so.
- The "intervention" must be well thought out, planned and practiced. A good counselor can accomplish this.
- Most children who are involved in gangs will need to be placed in a facility or out of state for several months.
- This may be very costly. A good counselor should be able to advise you on a cost-effective program.
- Join a parent support group such as "Tough Love." They are experienced in addressing out-of-control behavior.

Assessing: Self Esteem

My child:

_____ has poor eye contact

_____ seems pessimistic about most things

_____ has few friends

_____ rarely asserts him/herself

_____ avoids being praised

_____ has difficulty accepting gifts

_____ feels "less than" most children

_____ rarely asks for what he/she wants

Self esteem is what you believe about yourself and how you feel about it. All children benefit from Mom and Dad's praise and emotional support. What you say, don't say, do and don't do as a parent is under your child's watchful eye, twenty-four hours a day.

Self-Esteem Home Remedy

Stroke your child daily. Catch him/her being good and comment on it.

Attention. Spend time with your child everyday, even if it's just for a few minutes.

Listen to your child's feelings, not just the words. Reflect back on what you think he/she is feeling, for example, "You sound hurt to me."

U as in "I love u." Tell your child you love them every day. Don't assume they know you love them, say it.

Touch your child every day. Even older children need touch. This sends intimate messages necessary for emotional growth.

Eye contact, look your child in the eyes everyday. Eyes are the periscope of the soul. Eye contact sends your child warm, emotional energy.

Assessing: Substance Abuse

My child:

_____ has changes in grades (not necessarily failing grades)

_____ makes notations on notebooks/yearbooks mentioning drugs and alcohol

_____ has out of the ordinary mood-swings

_____ demonstrates drastic personality changes

_____ has had drug paraphernalia in his/her possession

_____ argues about alcohol, drugs or curfew violations

_____ is having school problems (truancy or suspensions, teacher arguments)

_____ has lost interest in activities that were once important to him/her

_____ has friends who have expressed concern over his/her alcohol or drug use

_____ has friends who are suspicious or he/she is being sneaky about his/her activities

If you checked off three or more or have suspicion that your child has a problem, don't deny your suspicion. If you think there is a problem, there probably is. Acknowledging a problem is fifty percent of the solution.

Substance Abuse Home Remedy

Addressing a substance abuse problem is one of the most difficult things for a parent to do. However, left unchecked it could result in a life-long problem. Therefore early intervention is a must.

1. Sit down with your child and level with them.

2. Use the Six Basic Feelings and reflections when discussing this problem with your child, i.e. "I found pot in your room. I feel afraid."

3. Make a written plan or thirty-day contract about trust.

Example:

You have violated our trust by using drugs. In order to resolve the problem and regain trust you must abide by the following contract:

- Professional assessment to determine the severity.
- Random drug/alcohol testing.
- Weekly family meeting to review specific progress.
- Banned from parties, concerts, or anywhere drugs are readily available.

If your child complies, revise the agreement month-to-month. If your child does not comply, seek professional treatment.

Assessing: Suicidal Tendencies

Be concerned if your child:

_____ writes about or makes mention of suicide

_____ has had a friend who committed or attempted suicide

_____ is giving away important possessions

_____ meets criteria for depression

_____ has a family history of suicide or attempts

_____ has lost all concern for self or others

_____ has friends who have expressed concern for his or her safety

_____ requests therapeutic help (to see a doctor or therapist)

_____ was depressed and all of sudden is happy for no apparent reason

Any and all hints of suicide should be taken seriously. Many times it's the child who threatens suicide as a manipulation who ends up going overboard, harming themselves, or even successfully committing suicide during an attention-seeking episode. If your child requests counseling, get it without delay.

Suicidal Tendencies Remedy

If you have observed two or more signs of suicidal tendency, get professional help immediately. If your child is willing to talk to you:

- Stay calm.
- Sit down with your child and express your love, as well as your concern about his/her moods.
- Tell him/her you are going to see a counselor.
- Tell your child you will stand by him/her through everything and for as long as it takes.

- Make a contract with your child agreeing not to harm him/herself.
- Monitor your child throughout the day and night before your counseling appointment.
- Follow through on the counseling appointment.

If your child is actively suicidal (about to attempt it now) call 911 or rush him/her to any emergency room. Police and psychiatrists have the authority to place your child on "psychiatric hold" and commit him/her to a psychiatric facility for up to seventy-two hours. A psychiatrist will evaluate the need for further treatment once your child is safely admitted to a treatment facility.

Appendix Two

Parents Contract Work Sheet

Five major concerns I have about my child are:

1.   _____

2.   _____

3.   _____

4.   _____

5.   _____

What I have done to handle each problem in the old way:

1.   _____

2.   _____

3.   _____

4.   _____

5.   _____

The results have been:

1.   _____

2.   _____

3.   _____

4.   _____

5.   _____

The new consequences I will use:

1. _____
2. _____
3. _____
4. _____
5. _____

Remember, consequences must always be in proportion to the offense. If you are concerned about your child's abuse of his iPod, you don't take away the computer; you take the iPod. "Keep it simple."

Citations

1. Smith, Christian. "Getting a Life," In Books & Culture, April, 2007.

2. Tompkins, Silvan. Referred to in Bradshaw, John. Healing the Shame that Binds. Health Communications, Inc., Publishers: Florida, 2005, pg. 4.

3. Bradshaw, John. Healing the Shame that Binds. Health Communications, Inc., Publishers: Florida, 2005, pg. 24.

4. Ibid, pg. 8.

5. Luthar, S.S., & C. Sexton, (2005), "The High Price of Affluence," in R. Kail (Ed.), Advances in Child Development. San Diego, CA: Academic Press.

6. Levine Ph.D., Madeline. The Price of Privilege. HarperCollins Publishers: New York, 2006, pg 66.

7. Black Ph.D., M.S.W., Claudia. Double Duty. Random House Publishers: New York, 1990, pg 7.

8. Bradshaw, John. Healing the Shame that Binds. Health Communications Inc.: Florida, 2005, pg. 68.

Remove the following page of the **Six Basic Feelings** from this book and display it for your family to see and refer to everyday when expressing their feelings

MAD
SAD
GLAD
AFRAID
ASHAMED
HURT

©Tim Chapman 1981

About the Author

Timothy Chapman, Msc.D., C.S.A.C.

Timothy Chapman is the founder and executive director of the Teensavers.com residential treatment program for adolescents, as well as Chapman House residential treatment program for adults in Southern California. He possesses thirty-years of experience working with teens, young adults and their parents. Timothy created the "Six-Basic Feelings" theory used exclusively at Chapman House and Teensavers as their foundational tool for recovery. He designed over ten treatment programs in California and opened the first adolescent outpatient treatment program in Hong Kong in 1994.

Timothy is a columnist for the Orange County Register Pulitzer Prize winning newspaper, a talk radio show host and he has consulted on many educational television projects.

As a Metaphysician, a professional Interventionist and a Certified Substance Abuse Counselor, Timothy has worked with thousands of families. His direct, teach by example approach has made him a leader in his field and America's Parenting Coach.